Where is Your Faith? Just Believe!

Faith Building Stories That Will Amaze and Astonish You

God also bore witness by signs and wonders and various miracles and by gifts of the Holy Spirit distributed according to His will.

Hebrews 2:4

Where is Your Faith? – Just Believe!

Published by Life Publications
www.lifepublications.org.uk
Cover design by Graham Alder

For further information go to:

www.healingroomscardiff.co.uk
Email:info@healingroomscardiff.co.uk

Tel: 0782 564 1970

Dedication

*This book is dedicated with my sincere gratitude to
You my Lord, through whom all things are possible.
You are worthy of all praise, honour and
glory both now and forever.*

Acknowledgements

I am grateful to You, Father, for my wife, Christalla.

Christalla, you are a true woman of God. Thank you for your unwavering love and support. I could never have done this without you.

I would like to thank all my brothers and sisters in Christ who contributed their testimonies to this book.

I would also like to thank Roy and Daphne Godwin of Ffald-y-Brenin Christian Retreat Centre, Arlette Frampton and Pastor Steve Ball (Senior Pastor of City Temple Church) for your advice and support.

Grateful thanks as well to Katrina Pettican for all her support.

A special thanks to David and Jan Holdaway for their guidance and expertise in helping to publish this book.

Commendations

Eighty-five years ago City Temple was birthed in a move of the Holy Spirit. Three thousand people were saved in fifty-one days and hundreds healed. The headlines in *The Daily Express* read, "Revival scenes in Cardiff." Ken Bailey's brilliant book reminds us that our God is the same yesterday, today and forever and that He still heals today. I encourage you to read this book with an open heart and allow God to stir your faith and expectation.

Thanks Ken for recording what God is going among us today and for increasing our hunger for another outpouring of the Holy Spirit.

Pastor Steve Ball
Senior Minister, Cardiff City Temple Church, Wales

I am so pleased to have the opportunity to write this introduction. Ken and his wife, Chrissie, first came to my attention in rather dramatic circumstances, as you will read a little later. Since then they have become friends and their on-going lives bear witness to a mighty God who is still able to save to the uttermost. His hand is not shortened. Neither is He at a loss when we call upon His name.

God has been moving for some time in releasing healing amongst many who visit Ffald-y-Brenin; it is what our forefathers referred to as a 'thin place', somewhere where the curtain between this world and heaven is gossamer thin. Nonetheless, no-one has ever been healed by Ffald-y-Brenin. It is through the mighty name of Jesus that healing flows.

The stories which follow will stir you up and encourage you to have faith that what God has done for others, He can do for you.

Authority, of course, does not lie in our stories. Rather, it lies in the word of God. Insofar as our experiences reflect the truth of the word, they are reliable as evidences; illustrations, if you like, of the dynamic truth of God. They encourage us that we are in the right road.

The testimonies herein bear witness to a number of biblical truths: that the Lord has deep compassion for us; that He hears our cries and feels our pain; that He does not ever abandon us but turns to us with overwhelming grace and mercy.

When Jesus said *'I will'*, touched the diseased, restored sight to the blind, opened deaf ears, caused the lame to walk, released the oppressed and proclaimed good news to the poor, He was only doing what the Father was doing and only spoke the words He heard His Father speaking. You can be fully confident in the promises of one who was sent to take up our pains and carry our suffering; by His stripes you are healed, (Isaiah 53:3-5).

I commend this book to you. May the day of the Lord's favour be refreshed to you as you read, and may the anointing power of the Holy Spirit cause you to be aflame with Him and for Him. And to Him be all the praise and glory!

Roy Godwin
Director, The Ffald-y-Brenin Trust
Co-author of the book The Grace Outpouring

Contents

Where is Your Faith? – Just Believe!

Foreword

The City Temple Church in Cardiff has a great legacy; it was founded by the great evangelist George Jeffreys. George's family were converted to Christ during the great Welsh Revival of 1904-1905.

George had a great anointing for preaching and the gift of faith for the miraculous. He travelled extensively throughout the UK and established many churches as a result of demonstrations of signs, wonders and miracles during his meetings.

In 1929 George visited Cardiff and rented a hall for what was expected to be two weeks of meetings. The hall was filled to capacity every night.

Other venues were hastily found to accommodate the thousands of people who wanted to hear and see George preach. At the end of a period of fifty one days, over three thousand people gave their lives to the Lord.

In 1934 the City Temple church was built in the heart of the city of Cardiff. The City Temple is just one of many Elim Pentecostal churches situated within the UK. It is a vibrant place of authentic and impassioned worship where people can encounter the life changing power of God.

Where is Your Faith? – Just Believe!

Introduction

'In mighty signs and wonders by the power of the spirit of God,'
(Romans15:16).

Amazement! Wide eyed, mouth agape, excitement.

I recall sitting in church with my mother and father and experiencing a warm, just eaten my favourite dessert, feeling in my stomach. It was sheer bliss for me to listen to the pastor recounting anecdotes about miracles he had seen in Africa. I was very young and loved to hear stories about extraordinary things. I was an avid reader of comics and fairy-tales and would daydream about being a super hero. However, even at that tender age I could differentiate between fact and fiction, dreams and reality. I truly believed that Jesus was real and I grew to love Him.

Whenever and wherever I heard the testimonies of Christian people illustrating God's amazing power at work in their lives, I would listen intently, mesmerised by those wondrous stories. I was so in awe of God. 1 John 5:9 tells us that that, *'If we receive the testimony of men, the testimony of God is greater, for this is the testimony of God that he has borne concerning His Son'.*

I am now a middle aged man and the passing years have not dimmed my enthusiasm to listen to others testify about supernatural encounters with God.

Where is Your Faith? – Just Believe!

Christian testimony builds and strengthens the faith of believers. James 2:17-18 says this, *'Faith by itself if not accompanied by action, is dead. But someone will say, Show me your faith: I have deeds. Show me your faith without deeds, and I will show you my faith by what I do.'*

Christians who share their faith with non-believers are giving them the wonderful opportunity of the gift of eternal life by testifying about the miraculous power of the Lord.

Psalm 118:46 talks about evangelising, *'I spoke of thy testimonies before kings; and was not ashamed.'*

Never the less, many believers find it difficult to share their supernatural experiences with non-believers because they are fearful of ridicule or perhaps worse. However, if we trust in the word of God the Holy Spirit will guide us and present us with opportunities to share the good news of the gospel of Jesus Christ. Isaiah 41:10 says, *'Fear not, for I am with you; do not be dismayed for I am your God, I will strengthen you and help you, I will uphold you with my righteous right hand.'*

Some Christian's have a 'Western world view' with regards to the supernatural workings of God. They willingly believe that miracles take place in far flung places such as the continents of Africa or Asia, but are doubtful that God would move in the same way in European countries. Spiritual things are deemed to be irrelevant to daily life, reality is defined by what can be seen, touched and measured, but God is not geographically limited He is omnipresent (everywhere at the same time) and is unchanged.

Other Christians believe miracles happen all the time because that is their experience and some believe miracles don't happen so often, because that's precisely what they see. There are also Christians who are sceptical about many of the testimonies they hear about miracles. Although they have a fundamental belief in moves of God they will only accept that they occur in unique situations; and those unique situations are rare.

Signs, wonders, healings and miracles that were performed in the Old and New Testament are still taking place today all over the world. Malachi 3:6 gives us this divine assurance, '*I am the Lord, I do not change.*'

In many developing nations the life experience of the vast majority is grinding poverty. They have poor infrastructures, insufficient provision of medical services and finite resources of food and water.

God is the one those individuals turn to for help because there is no one else who can solve their problems. How He does it transcends their human comprehension but regardless of this they are obedient to God because the scripture says, '*Trust in the Lord with all your heart and do not lean on your own understanding,*' (Proverbs 3:5). These disadvantaged people trust in the promise that says that they can '*cast all their anxiety on Him because He cares for you,*' (1 Peter 5:7).

God will often put us in situations where we are given the option to make a choice whether or not to put our trust in Him. How many of us seek God prior to consulting others in times of trouble? How many phone friends and family for advice or visit the doctor or dentist when the symptoms first appear?

I am not advocating that we do not do these things, which in essence are good and often necessary. For example, going to the doctor is okay and is often the wise thing to do, because the Lord may ask us to do what the doctor requires of us until He brings us to full recovery. However, if we talk to God prior to doing anything about our problems, He can calm our anxieties, eradicate fear, miracles can happen, doors can open, healings can take place. Psalm 28:7 says, '*The Lord is my strength and my shield; in Him my heart trusts, and I am helped*'.

Our God is the God of the impossible and He wants to glorify Himself through the demonstration of His power. All the contributors to this book attest to this truth given that they have been touched by the Lord in one way or another. I felt moved by God to compile these testimonies to glorify His precious name.

Dear reader, I trust that your faith will be strengthened as mine has been by seeing lives transformed and people set free through the manifestation of God's divine love and miraculous power.

1

Christalla Bailey

I was a divorced, professional man, in my late forties, living independently in a modest two bedroom house in a quiet suburb in Cardiff, South Wales. I wasn't a native of Cardiff having been born and raised in Gloucester, England. I had moved to Cardiff from Suffolk as part of a relocation arrangement with my employer, the Probation Service. I made the decision to move to Wales following the breakdown of my marriage in 2006. I felt reasonably happy with my lot, but if I had been really honest with myself I was lonely and felt a spiritual void in my life.

During weekdays I had no time to be introspective; I was far too busy working and undertaking keep fit pursuits during the evenings. However, during the weekends my loneliness intensified. In the supermarket, coffee shop, town centre, in fact, wherever I went, there seemed to be couples just about everywhere. Saturdays were bad enough but Sundays were excruciating, not least on sunny days. Couples strolling in the sunshine, walking hand in hand, whilst looking into each other's eyes, were the most annoying.

Nevertheless, I chose not to rectify the situation due to my romantic ideal that when the time was right the right person would come along. Besides, how would I meet someone? I didn't frequent nightclubs or trendy pubs. I felt that I was far too long in the tooth for that. I had contemplated trying Internet dating but believed that that was for 'sad' people, and certainly beneath me! I'd heard all the horror stories and decided that I would give that particular mode of meeting eligible females a wide berth.

My arrogance was simply pretence. In reality, I didn't think that I was desirable. I was almost fifty years of age and not getting any younger. My daughters, Tara and Tanya, would often mention my singleton status and discuss strategies to match me up with a nice lady. Tanya extolled the virtues of Internet dating but Tara was utterly opposed to the idea, she felt I should do things the conventional way.

A few months later, I was working on my computer and decided to have a brief look at a dating website. A couple of clicks was all it took to join the legions of individuals searching for their prospective dream partner.

The website had a free sample gallery which allowed the viewer to browse prior to deciding whether or not to sign up for membership. The first picture I saw was of a beautiful dark haired woman whose name was Christalla. I stared in disbelief whilst several thoughts raced through my head. I recall exclaiming the word 'wow' and thinking 'why is she single?' I convinced myself that this process was a ruse devised to trick hapless males into parting with their hard earned cash and consoled myself with the notion that 'she wouldn't look twice at me.' I promptly clicked the exit button.

During the next few days I attempted to erase the image of Christalla from my mind but to no avail. Besides the fact that she was very attractive there was something about her that intrigued me. I fought the impulse to re-visit the dating site (*I really did try, honestly*) but eventually succumbed to my curiosity. On this occasion I looked at the finer details of what Christalla had written in her profile, just in case this was a genuine contact.

What I read appeared to be legitimate, but one thing in particular struck a chord. She was interested in meeting a Christian man. I reached for my credit card.

I had been brought up in the Seventh Day Adventist Church. When I was aged eighteen, I decided to leave the church. I felt that the God I had loved as a child had become distant. In my mind He was overly stern and wanted to take all the fun out of life. I wanted to enjoy my youth, unencumbered by the rigidity of the suffocating 'rules and regulations' of church life.

On reflection I believe that I was still grieving for my mother whom the Lord called home when I was twelve years old. I missed her terribly and was angry with God for taking her from me.

I began to walk 'in the flesh' and entered a wilderness of sin and carnality. For many years I did not pray or read the bible and developed an interest in visiting clairvoyants and mediums. However, despite my sinful and wayward ways God was always with me. On every occasion that I encountered a major problem in my life, I would call out to Him for help and He would provide the solution.

It was not until I was in my mid-thirties that I decided to try and find a place of worship. I needed Christian fellowship. I didn't want to return to the church I had attended in my formative years because I felt that their doctrines were too conservative. I began to visit a number of churches in my vicinity but couldn't find one that stirred my soul. Eventually my enthusiasm waned and I lost interest.

When Christalla and I met for the first time the chemistry between us was incredible. I was immediately smitten. She had the most beautiful dark hair and large expressive eyes. She was extremely humorous and clearly had a zest for life. At the end of our first date I was really thrilled that she was interested in me and wanted to meet with me again.

During the subsequent weeks our relationship developed and we discovered that we had a few things in common. For example we were both born of immigrant parents, had two children, were former business owners, and had previously been married.

My parents were Jamaican and Christalla's parents were Greek Cypriot. Christalla was christened into the Greek Orthodox Church and was taken to church every Easter and Christmas. Although her first language is Greek she could never understand the teachings as the tradition is for the priests to read the scripture in classical Greek.

At the age of ten Christalla entered the family business, Constantinou Hairdressers. She was fully trained by the age of fourteen and running one of her father's salons by the age of sixteen. The Constantinou's are well known in Cardiff as they are champion hairdressers and have several salons in various parts of the city. Christalla developed a passion for dance and embarked upon a career as a professional dancer. She later decided to settle down and get married at the age of twenty-three and had two children; Irene and Phil.

Christalla had divorced an abusive husband and was not in the best of health. She disclosed that she suffered with a condition known as Myalgic Encephalomyelitis (M.E.) and had done so for over two decades. Christalla contracted M.E. after a bout of glandular fever following the birth of her first child Irene. So as a consequence she had been unable to work for many years due to the disabling effects of this condition.

I had never heard of M.E. but recalled a newspaper article I'd read several years prior which profiled investment traders, bankers and innovative business owners and dubbed them as 'yuppies' (young upwardly mobile professionals).

These individuals had all become inexplicably afflicted with a mystery illness which became known as 'yuppie flu'.

I remembered how the article reported (with what appeared to be a huge relish) the demise of these high fliers.

I was completely bemused by this disclosure given Christalla's healthy and robust appearance. She told me that the vast majority of M.E. sufferers were subject to scepticism and discrimination. Sadly, this was the attitude of the medical profession, from whom M.E. sufferers needed the most understanding.

Many doctors, scientists and researchers deem the illness to be psychosomatic rather than a physical condition. This is despite the existence of countless documented case histories of people suffering with this condition. M.E. is documented by the World Health Organisation as an illness of a physical cause, a neurological condition.

There are approximately twenty million M.E. sufferers worldwide. Treatment for M.E. in the UK is not widely available via the National Health Service (NHS). Many have to source treatment from private specialist clinics, invariably at great cost and/or via complimentary therapies.

Christalla's illness birthed a desire within her to explore alternative therapies and faiths in her search for the meaning of life, health and healing. Most of the therapies she tried would ease her symptoms but only for a short period of time. Aside from not being healed Christalla was always left with a void in her spirit, she knew there was more. Then one day Christalla visited Thornhill Community Centre. As soon as she entered the building she felt a peaceful presence, something that she had never previously experienced. Christalla didn't know what the presence was but she knew that her search was over, she had found what she was looking for. Christalla later discovered that the building was also used as a church and was curious to know more, so signed up for the *Alpha* course.

Where is Your Faith? – Just Believe!

During the early part of the course Christalla was very sceptical and continually asked questions. However, at the half way point there was a huge awakening within her, Christalla knew she was hearing truth. One of the *Alpha* leaders introduced her to a woman who had Fibromyalgia and they became friends. One day Christalla saw her friend and almost didn't recognise her because she looked so different. Christalla asked her friend what had happened to her. Her friend told her that Jesus had healed her. At that precise moment Christalla accepted Jesus as her personal Saviour

Christalla invited me to attend her church in Thornhill, North Cardiff. I asked her if I should wear a suit but was surprised when she said, 'Jeans will be fine.' Attending church wearing jeans would have been unheard of in the church I grew up in, so I decided to err on the side of caution and dressed casually in a cotton shirt and flannel trousers. 'At least I won't be too scruffy,' I thought.

As we approached the doors of the church I felt distinctly underdressed but was reassured to be welcomed by a kindly gentleman who was similarly attired. He possessed a genuinely warm smile and (perhaps due to my deficiencies in that area) I was particularly impressed by his full head of wavy hair which was as white as snow.

By the end of the service I was feeling uplifted and inspired. I wanted more of the same so continued to attend Thornhill church with Christalla.

Although Christalla really enjoyed going to her local church she encouraged me to visit other places of worship to allow me the opportunity to decide if I would prefer to attend church elsewhere.

The first church we visited was an experience to say the least. Towards the end of the service the pastor asked people to come forward for intercession, prayer and the laying on of hands.

Encouraged by Christalla I left my seat and waited expectantly in line. I watched quizzically as the pastor seemed to be scything through a corn field as each person he touched fell to the floor. Suddenly it was my turn!

The pastor placed his hand on my chest. I waited for a moment expecting to feel my knees to buckle.

Nothing happened!

I vividly recall the look of bemusement in the pastor's eyes as I remained standing and the pursing of his lips whilst he took a deep breath, and prepared to push me to the floor. Suffice to say the pastor was unsuccessful because I stood my ground and didn't give an inch. Suitably annoyed, I returned to my seat.

Shortly afterwards Christalla came towards me shaking her head from side to side with a 'can't believe what has just happened' look on her face. She told me with much indignation that the pastor had also tried to push her to the floor.

'I was having none of it,' Christalla said rather triumphantly. As I was in deep contemplation about the implications of this experience, I was brought back to full consciousness by the loud sound of a gong. It was being repeatedly bashed by a rather enthusiastic young man who was running to and fro along the aisles of the church. We promptly left.

I had seen several television documentaries which featured people 'falling down in the spirit' and speaking in tongues. I had been distinctly underwhelmed by it all. I wanted to believe that it was a genuine phenomenon but was very sceptical. This experience increased my scepticism.

A while later, Christalla and I visited a Sunday morning service at a Pentecostal church called the City Temple. The church is situated in the centre of Cardiff. I was amazed at the size of auditorium and also how many people were in the congregation.

I couldn't see any empty seats on the lower levels but spotted a few in the upper tiers.

Christalla's energy levels were very low so I held onto her hand tightly and literally dragged her up the steps behind me. This was how we would tackle stairs if a stairlift or lift was not available.

The service was already underway with a rousing worship song. The congregation was singing with lots of joyful gusto, many with their hands raised the air.

At the end of the fourth song the pastor stepped onto the podium and asked the congregation to be seated to prepare to partake in communion. At that precise moment something which I can only describe as an energy-surge entered my body. I felt as if I wanted to float out of my seat. I panicked. I began to weep (but not with sadness) and then grasped the seat with my right hand and Christalla with my left. I wanted to shout at the top of my voice with joy but suppressed the urge to do so. I was already embarrassed about my behaviour and couldn't face the thought of what I imagined would be further disapproval.

Even though I was worshipping amongst charismatic Christians the conservatism of my church upbringing was indelibly stamped upon my psyche. Spontaneous outbursts were not encouraged in the church I grew up in. Falling down in the spirit? Speaking in tongues? That sort of conduct would not have been tolerated.

When I later reflected on what had transpired at the church, I thought I'd had some sort of panic attack. However, when Christalla explained what had actually taken place, that I had been touched by the Holy Spirit, I was euphoric. All my doubts were swept away! God's hand was upon me. I decided then and there that this was the church for me. I wanted more, I was so excited.

Christalla knew that following this experience it was unlikely that I would want to join her church, so we discussed the practicalities of a move. Christalla's condition would invariably trigger a boost of energy late in the evening or night and would cause heavy fatigue in the morning. This extreme tiredness was a consequence of her body's mismanagement of a naturally produced chemical known as cortisol. It would literally take her two hours to get ready for church and if she was rushed, her body would seize up. In addition to this the logistics of travel were also a problem. On a Sunday morning I would have had to drive from the south of Cardiff to the north of the city and back again as my house was fairly close to the City Temple.

Given this situation it would be very difficult for us to arrive at the City Temple on time for Sunday worship. I was also conscious that Christalla had attended her church for several years and had made many friends there. We decided to maintain our attendance of Thornhill church, which I was pleased to do.

Christalla and I were encouraged to join a home group which took place a couple of miles from her home. A few months later we attended a Christmas party there. During the evening each person was asked to draw a folded piece of paper from a basket. Each piece of paper had a scripture verse written on it. Christalla chose Mark 11: 24-26. The verses tell us that whatever we ask for we will receive, if we believe, and continue to say that if we hold anything against anyone we should forgive them, as our Father in heaven forgives us. Christalla took the paper home and stuck it on her wardrobe so that she could look at it every day to remind her of how important it was to practice belief and forgiveness in her daily walk with God.

Our relationship blossomed and I fell deeply in love with Christalla. It was during a wonderful holiday in Spain that I spontaneously asked Christalla to marry me. I was so happy when she accepted but there was a slight problem...the ring...I didn't have one!

The next day was spent visiting jewellery shops and, ironically, a Catholic priest gave us directions to the shop we eventually bought the ring from.

When we returned to Wales the problems began. Two days prior to our engagement party Christalla broke her arm. Given that she was intolerant to all conventional medication (even an aspirin) she had to cope without pain killers. I was so proud of her, she never complained once. That was bad enough one would have thought, however, when she told her mother that we were engaged to be married, she disowned Christalla. Her mother disliked me because of the colour of my skin and hoped that her daughter's relationship with me would flounder. From then on things got progressively worse.

During the following eighteen months Christalla's health deteriorated alarmingly. She suffered terribly with pain, fatigue, sleepless nights, fainting spells, heart and respiratory problems. On two occasions she almost died when the oxygen levels in her body fell so dangerously low.

As a couple we encountered some gut wrenching periods of suffering, our savings were swallowed up on treatments and associated expenses, and we also had to postpone our wedding which really tested our faith.

No matter what difficulties Christalla faced she would never grumble. Her faith never wavered for one moment. Mine did. I even considered turning my back on God. Christalla was such an example to me.

During one of my pity parties she said, 'Who are you going to turn to if you haven't got God? There is nowhere else to go.'

She was absolutely correct. What was I thinking! I should have been the one giving spiritual encouragement to her, not the reverse.

It was January 2010. 'Enough is enough!' Christalla exclaimed loudly. 'I have to find a solution to this (health) problem. I can't go on like this.'

Christalla had spent the majority of the two years prior to her healing in bed because of the severity of her condition. She couldn't keep her balance even whilst sitting in a chair. She couldn't digest food, and as a consequence, lost weight at an alarming rate. Christalla struggled to get to the toilet, was in constant pain, she had virtually no memory retention, poor brain function and no muscle strength. To compound matters further, she was allergic to chemicals, including deodorants and perfume, and had multiple food allergies and intolerances.

At the very moment I was writing this paragraph Christalla's teddy bear; which holds a cushion with the words 'God Cares' emblazoned upon it, flew off the shelf (it didn't simply fall) and landed on the floor. Wow! Thank You for loving us Lord!

Christalla began to research the internet for information regarding innovative treatments for M.E. sufferers. She came across the privately run Breakspear Clinic, in Hemel Hempstead, England. Our strategy was to get an assessment at the clinic and then we would apply to get funding for treatment through the NHS. There was a slight problem however, we couldn't afford the consultation fee of two hundred and fifty pounds. Christalla and I decided to pray fervently for God to provide a solution.

During the week I would occasionally visit St John's Church which is in the city centre close to my office. I would often go there to find solace and spend time with God.

On this particular day I tried to ring Christalla just prior to entering the church to inform her I was going to pray for us. However, her phone was engaged.

I went in regardless and asked God for an answer to our funding problem. When I left the church, I decided to ring Christalla again.

'I tried to ring you earlier, who was that on the phone?' I asked. She told me excitedly that a friend had offered to pay the consultation fee for the clinic. The offer of money had taken place during my prayer to the Lord. Amazing!

A couple of weeks later we visited the Breakspear clinic and following the consultation were told that it was going to cost an additional £750 for a medical evaluation. The assessment of Christalla's condition was to be made by consultant Dr Julu. We were informed that the process involved the use of an Autonomic Analysis machine which evaluates the level of chemical and physical anomalies in the body. We discovered that these machines are utilised by the health service in Denmark but not in the UK. Evidently, only a handful of private hospitals and clinics within the UK have access to these machines.

We did some research on the Breakspear clinic. The clinic appeared to have a good reputation and Dr Julu's credentials were impeccable. We also read the affidavits of many of the clinic's M.E. patients on line, who had been treated successfully by the clinic. Bolstered by these good reports we stepped out in faith and made the booking, trusting that God would provide.

A couple of weeks later I received an unexpected tax rebate which covered the cost of the evaluation at the clinic. God knew that our savings would have had to be used for the consultation fee and gave us a gift to avoid us doing so. Thank you Lord!

The Autonomic test results confirmed that Christalla was very ill and needed extensive treatment which would cost thousands of pounds. We continued to pray for healing, and asked for guidance. We applied for funding from the Local Health Board.

Our application was denied. We then requisitioned an advocate to act on our behalf to make an appeal. The appeal was declined.

As Christalla's health steadily worsened, my prayers intensified. In desperation, I cried out to God.

During this time Christalla was largely bed bound and only ventured outside of her home to attend home group and church. Although Christalla would insist on attending City Temple every Sunday, her immune system was too weak to cope with the deodorants, perfumes and colognes worn by between four to five hundred people. I often had to carry her out before the end of the services because was so ill, much to her embarrassment. Christalla told me that she knew that she was in a spiritual battle and that, 'something was trying to fix her and something was trying to take her out.' She said that although she did not have a thorough knowledge of the Bible she would use the word of God when her situation became unbearable and things would ease and get better for a while.

Whilst praying for the full restoration of Christalla's health I referred to the scriptures and in particular Luke 8:43-48 which tells the story of the woman who suffered for twelve years being healed by her faith.

I told God that Christalla had incredible faith too and had been an inspiration to me during her suffering by demonstrating an unwavering belief in His love and power to heal. I asked God to grant Christalla the opportunity to reach out and symbolically touch Jesus' garment because she truly believed that her body would be healed if she did so.

I often visualised myself carrying Christalla on my back, pushing through the throng, sweat pouring from my body as I strained every sinew to get as close as possible to Jesus before setting her down to enable her make those last few steps and reach out in faith.

I petitioned God so many times, asking for healing, that I would often simply say, 'Father, you know what is in my heart…'

When we pray the Lord knows what we are going to ask, so I thought it best not to bore Him by too much repetition. Joking aside, perseverance and persistence in prayer does bring results. James 5:16 tells us that fervent prayers are powerful and effective.

During my daily devotional time with the Lord, I had a deep conviction that He would answer my prayers for Christalla to be healed. God had spoken to me in my spirit in 2008 and told me that Christalla would be healed. It wasn't a matter of… will God heal Christalla…it was a matter of when.

During a conversation with Christalla about the healing power of Jesus she said that she'd had a vision about the story of the woman who was healed by faith when she touched the edge of His garment. I was amazed by this disclosure given that I had not previously told her about the specific details of my prayers.

References to this biblical story began to appear seemingly everywhere. In the midst of a sermon at church, during a conversation with a Christian friend, seven times in total. Christalla ordered a Christian healing CD from the USA and the first scripture referred mentioned was? You guessed it; Luke 8:43.

Christalla and I attended a Wednesday evening home group meeting and the teaching focussed (surprise, surprise) on the woman with the blood issue. Christalla and I were astonished that this anecdote had come to the fore again. We knew that this continued reference to Luke 8 was pertinent but as yet we hadn't had our eyes opened to its significance. We explained to the group how we were both drawn to this woman's encounter with Jesus and someone said, 'Perhaps God is telling you that you need to step out in faith'. Christalla suddenly recalled something that caused her to gasp loudly!

It was in the preceding year that Christalla received the gift of a book from her friend Linda Tatham. The book was entitled 'The Grace Outpouring' written by Roy Godwin and Dave Roberts. The story is of a Christian retreat centre in West Wales known as Ffald-y-Brenin where amazing things had taken place. God was moving mightily in this place. The book illustrated many occurrences of divine healings, people having incredible encounters with God and lives being transformed.

At that time Christalla attempted to book a short stay but the retreat was fully booked. She was unable to book in advance due to being unable to predict whether or not her fluctuating illness would inhibit travel. Christalla therefore decided to try again when she felt a little better.

Christalla told the home group members that she had suddenly understood that God had been using the story in Luke 8 to encourage her to take a leap of faith and that perhaps Ffald-y-Brenin was the symbolic edge of Christ's garment.

Two days later I attended a Christian men's weekend in a Christian retreat in Llanmadog, West Wales. This was my first experience of this type of event which was ironically called the 'escape weekend'. It was a great opportunity to spend time with other Christians and also enjoy fun filled events. Given how ill Christalla had been I was reluctant to attend but she encouraged me to do so to give me a chance for some respite.

I was deeply moved by Christalla's compassion for me in the midst of her suffering. She was worried that I was on the verge of a nervous breakdown. There were also concerns about her son Phil who was having panic and anxiety attacks. Christalla's daughter, Irene, and family friend, Liz, offered to deputise and look after her whilst I was away. I accepted the offers, I was exhausted.

Where is Your Faith? – Just Believe!

I rang Christalla several times a day throughout the weekend to check that everything was okay. She told me that she was being well looked after and insisted that I relax and enjoy myself.

I returned to Cardiff on Sunday evening eagerly looking forward to seeing Christalla. When I arrived at her house she was upstairs in bed. As I entered her bedroom my heart sank. Her skin had the pallor of grey and her eyes looked dull and tired. I knelt beside her bed and put my arms around her. She looked so frail and vulnerable.

'I was carried out of church this morning,' she whispered, almost apologetically. Christalla told me that she had hardly slept throughout the weekend because of respiratory and heart problems.

I am ashamed to admit that I became enraged by this news. I had just spent a wonderful weekend with other Christian men glorifying God's name, yet my fiancée's health had worsened. I told Christalla that I needed a 'word' with God and went out for a walk.

For half an hour I ranted and raved as I marched around the streets. I cried out, 'You are a healing God! Scripture says so! I believe in you…Christalla believes in you…The bible says that if we abide in your word and you abide in us, we can ask anything of you…We believe your word so why won't you heal her? You told me that you would heal her a long time ago, I believed that I'd heard from you. If that was truly your voice I heard, why don't you heal her? We are at the end of our tether, she can't take any more, I can't take anymore. I don't know if I have the strength to carry on.

'I know we have to be patient because everything you do is in your time, not ours, but I don't want to bury her, I want to marry her… You have to act now, she is slipping away… Please help us!'

When I returned to the house I was spent. I had prayed with such fervour and intensity that I had got rid of all the anger and frustration from my system and become rational again. I prayed with Christalla and went to the spare room to go to bed. I was ashamed of the way I had spoken to God and asked for His forgiveness. After praying, I still felt embarrassed about shouting at the Lord so it took quite a while to fall asleep.

In the morning Christalla told me she had had the best night rest for days! I praised God for His love and mercy. Hearing this from Christalla gave me hope. Was God doing something? I felt relieved that perhaps God was not angry with me for 'standing in the gap' for Christalla in the way that I had during the previous evening. However, as a precaution I apologised again.

I later discovered from conversations with other Christians who were a little more mature in their walk with the Lord that sometimes it is okay to get angry with God (in the right way of course). He understands the struggles we go through in life and is receptive to 'aggressive' petitioning when the situation warrants it. God sends the Holy Spirit to help us in expressing ourselves in harmony with His will by praying for us, (Romans 8:26-27).

I went to work on Monday morning then drove back to Christalla's house that evening to be with her. I decided to take the Tuesday as a day's leave which was unusual for me as this was always such a busy day at work, but I just couldn't concentrate.

Christalla told me that when she realised that her vision of the woman in Luke 8 was about a leap of faith, she decided to conduct some research into Ffald-y-Brenin. She told me that she had discovered that on Tuesday, October 4, (which was the next day), there was scheduled a day of worship.

Christalla asked what I thought about driving her there. Without considering the implications of what she was actually asking me

31

to do, I said, 'I don't mind.' Even though I said this, Christalla was still unsure about what to do. We decided that if she managed to get a good night's rest we would travel, if not, we would stay put.

In the morning Christalla told me that she had a disturbed night. Having slept badly seemed to motivate her. 'Let's go to Ffald-y-Brenin,' she exclaimed boldly, 'I really want to go.'

I was worried.

The last time we'd travelled a long distance, Christalla's skin had turned blue due to her oxygen levels dropping dramatically following a heart malfunction. The medics told me that if they had been a few minutes later arriving at the scene, Christalla would have been dead. When we phoned Dr Julu to relay to him what had happened, he was livid. He told us that travelling was far too dangerous for Christalla and gave her strict instructions not to attempt any further travel.

Two months prior to this incident Christalla had attempted to travel to an organic food festival which was taking place in Bristol. Christalla and I attended this festival every year.

This was a treat for her because virtually all the food Christalla ate was organic but also because we would invariably return home with a car laden with 'freebies'. We both knew that travel wasn't advisable but given the good weather forecast we decided to take a risk and make the journey. The trip usually took around an hour. The plan was that following our arrival Christalla would remain in her wheelchair throughout the time we were there. During previous trips she would walk some of the way, rest and if needs be, use the wheelchair.

The best laid plans? We got caught in a traffic jam during the journey and Christalla became very poorly. The heat was unbearable and the air conditioning in the car was malfunctioning. I quickly pulled off the main carriageway, lifted

Christalla out of the car onto a blanket and lay her on the hard shoulder of the motorway.

I was frantic with worry and rang the emergency services. Christalla's heart was struggling to cope with the heat and the fumes would eventually begin to cause breathing problems. However, during that awful situation, God demonstrated that He was with us, He was still in control.

A pick-up truck towing a car came slowly towards us on the hard shoulder. The driver put his indicator on to signal that he wanted to get back onto the main carriageway so that he could negotiate his way around my car. I watched as the truck passed us and noticed that when it was a few yards away from us it turned sharply off the motorway. I hadn't noticed that our car was a short distance from a large open area which led to a slip road. I immediately put Christalla back in the car and drove off the carriageway. I opened every door in the vehicle to keep her cool whilst we waited for the medics. A short while later help arrived and Christalla was taken to hospital. As I followed the ambulance I realised that where I had positioned the car had saved us valuable time. The next exit from the motorway was several miles away.

So, when Christalla informed me that it would take two and a quarter hours to get to Ffald-y-Brenin and the scheduled prayer service was of five hours duration, I was beside myself with indignation and fear.

'You cannot go, you're not well enough to travel that far and cope with such a long a day,' I said. 'It's a crazy idea.'

Christalla, who has always had great insight and wisdom, looked me in the eye and said, 'Where is your faith?'

I was shaken to the core, she was absolutely right. Where was my faith? By refusing to take Christalla to Ffald-y-Brenin I would be submitting to fear instead of trusting in the Lord. Fear is not of

God. In 2 Timothy1:7 it says, *'God has not given us a spirit of fear, but power, and of love, and of a sound mind.'*

I felt a sense of shame because under the pretext of concern for Christalla, I had allowed myself to be used by the enemy to try and put doubt in Christalla's mind.

Suitably chastised I prepared to travel but my heart bled as I watched her descend in the stair lift, this was a forty five year old woman for goodness sake!

Once we were settled in the car, Christalla tapped the postcode of our destination into the satellite navigation unit but it was malfunctioning. This was confusing given that it was a fairly new piece of equipment which hadn't presented us with a problem previously. We were already behind schedule due to my reluctance to travel, so this was the last thing we needed.

Christalla switched the machine on and off several times in an attempt to re-boot it, but to no avail. She turned to me and said, 'This is confirmation that I should go, the enemy is trying to stop us getting there.'

We prayed aloud for God to assist us. Christalla pressed the on/off switch again. Amazingly, it sprang into life.

His is the greater power, above all else, in the heavenly and earthly realms. Thank You, Father.

Shortly after beginning the journey Christalla pulled a CD from her bag and asked if I would mind if she played it. I agreed and asked if I had heard it previously. 'No, you probably haven't,' she said. 'It's new, there are some lovely tracks on it.'

As Christalla slotted the disc into the player I noticed that her hand was shaking. Whenever her hands shook this was an indication that she was really struggling. She was clearly not well enough to travel. I took a deep breath and supressed my natural inclination to dissuade her from continuing the journey.

The worship songs had a calming effect on me and I began to listen to the lyrics. In one of the refrains, the singer sang '…meet me by the river, by the river I will be waiting to cleanse you from your despair.'

The message was incredibly poignant and Christalla began to weep. I assumed she was crying because of her situation and the lyric. Christalla sensed what I was thinking and said, 'I am not sad, I don't know why but I just can't stop crying.'

We arrived at least half an hour late and were surprised by the large number of cars parked on either side of the country lane leading to the chapel.

We didn't realise it at the time but we were not in Ffald-y-Brenin, we were in the village of Cwm Gwaun which is about a five minute drive from the retreat. As we got out of the car we were comforted to see others who were also arriving belatedly for the service. Christalla and I had that smug smile on our faces that said, 'At least we're not the only ones who are going to be embarrassed when we walk in.'

The setting was stunning. The little whitewashed chapel was surrounded by hills, fields and woods.

Christalla and I slowly made our way towards the chapel. When we got inside Roy Godwin was already addressing the congregation. A kindly gentleman quietly ushered us to the back of the room and chairs were hurriedly found for us.

The chapel seemed to be bursting at the seams. There were probably no less than a hundred people there. Roy continued to speak for a short while then he paused to say something that I will never…ever…forget.

'I have just been given a word, that there is a person in the congregation who has travelled here seeking healing. They have been crying out, night after night in desperation. The message is; it is done, you are healed.'

Christalla and I looked at each other excitedly. I knew that we were thinking the exact same thing. Could it be her that God was speaking to?

We both scanned the room trying to detect signs of acknowledgement. No hands were raised, no one appeared to be staking a claim. We remained silent. I knew that at that precise moment we were both offering up a fervent prayer in our hearts.

A little later in the service Roy separated the congregation into prayer groups each consisting of four people. Christalla and I were paired with a delightful couple from the East Midlands who had been staying at the Ffald-y-Brenin retreat for a few days. We shared our story with them and they enthusiastically encouraged us to speak to Roy. They were convinced that Christalla was the one that God had sent the message to. *'He sent His word and healed them,'* (Psalm 107:20).

During the coffee break Christalla and I plucked up the courage to speak to Roy. I was struck by the way his eyes smiled as he greeted us. He listened to Christalla's account of years of ill health and her utter conviction that if she journeyed to Ffald-y-Brenin she would be healed. Roy intimated that no one else had come forward to claim the message of healing and said that he felt that Christalla was clearly the one God had been talking to.

Roy asked if he could bless us both. I was intrigued by this request. In the past I had been asked many times if I wanted prayer but never a blessing. He was being courteous by asking but there was no need, we were so pleased that he wanted to do that for us. Roy placed a hand on each of our heads and declared God's blessing upon us both.

Roy had been joyful and appreciative that we had spoken to him but didn't appear to be surprised by what had happened. We were curious, then later discovered that there was a simple explanation for this. Miracles and manifestations of healing had been commonplace at Ffald-y-Brenin for years. What had happened to us was simply a continuance of God's redemptive love for those that sought Him there.

Just prior to commencing the second half of the service Roy gave an account of our three-way conversation to the congregation and proclaimed that 'God is good.'

At the end of the service we made the five minute journey up to the Ffald-y-Brenin retreat. It is a truly beautiful, peaceful sanctuary. It is often described as a 'thin place,' a place where heaven meets earth.

We visited the chapel and then walked along the bridal path which leads to what is known as the 'high cross.' The timber cross is positioned on the edge of a cliff overlooking the valley. Christalla and I stood beneath the rugged structure and thanked God for His mercy and grace. The world stood still for me. I felt peace. I felt God's presence.

During the journey home Christalla told me that when we arrived at Ffald-y-Brenin that morning she felt really unwell and her heart had begun to beat wildly.

She decided not to say anything to me because she knew I would have panicked. Christalla recounted how she had remonstrated with herself and said, 'What am I doing? I'm in the middle of nowhere, the nearest hospital is miles away, I am feeling very ill and am not sure I will make it through the next few minutes, much less the day.'

The enormity of what she had done in travelling to Ffald-y-Brenin had suddenly become apparent. She trusted in the Lord and surrendered herself totally to Him by saying, 'God, I am in your hands now.'

I asked her how she felt. She said, 'Fine.'

Where is Your Faith? – Just Believe!

I smiled and thanked God in my heart for giving Christalla the strength to cope with the rigours of the day. I realised that she had been rewarded for her faith. Hebrews 11:1 tells us that *'faith is the assurance of things hoped for, the conviction of things not seen.'*

When we got back to Christalla's house we had a light supper and retired to our separate rooms; Christalla's room was upstairs and mine was on the ground floor.

The following day I awoke at around 8.30am and routinely climbed the stairs to ask Christalla what she would like for breakfast. I pushed the door open and the bed was empty. I retraced my steps and gently knocked on the doors of her children's rooms. No response.

I checked every other room of the house but she was nowhere to be seen. I became concerned because I couldn't understand what was happening. I was beginning to think the worst. Perhaps the medics had been summoned by Christalla's children during the night and no-one had woken me.

I went downstairs into the kitchen with the intent of going into the garden through the outhouse. Then the outhouse door opened. In walked Christalla, fully dressed and wearing a coat!

'Where have you been?' I spluttered in relief.
'For a walk.'
'But...but how... you can't walk unaided?'

'I'm healed!' she shouted, punching the air. 'I woke up early. I was full of energy and just had an urge to get out into the fresh air. I walked through the fields praising God and was amazed by how green the fields are. Everything looks so different. Praise God, thank You Lord!'

Whilst out walking Christalla realised that when she had been weeping in the car during the journey to Ffald-y-Brenin, she was being anointed, the healing process had begun. The completion of

38

this compassionate act of God came when she said. 'I am in your hands now.'

She had laid everything at God's throne of grace. She had stepped out in faith, completely trusting in God. She truly believed that He was greater than what she was facing, that He understood her suffering and was able to bring redemption to the situation. Her faith opened a channel through which God's healing and restoration flowed.

Christalla's heart beating at an abnormal rate was a sign of over exertion. Once this happened her heart would not regulate and she would faint. A frantic phone call for medical assistance would invariably follow. However, after Roy had spoken, Christalla's heart slowed down, something that had never happened previously. It was at this moment that she sensed that healing was taking place. Her mind was also taken back to the journey to Ffald-y-Brenin that morning when she had been weeping uncontrollably in the car. Christalla said that she felt as if something had completely taken over and all she could do was surrender to it.

'Blessed are those who have not seen yet believe,' (John 20:29). Proverbs 4:7 says, *'My son (daughter) be attentive to my words; incline your ear to my sayings. Let them not escape from your sight; keep them within your heart for they are life to those who find them, and healing to their flesh.'*

Christalla did not let God's truth escape from her sight or her heart. He blessed her abundantly for her belief in Him. He said, *'Daughter, your faith has made you well, go in peace,'* (Luke 8:48).

Thank You Father, Praise Your Holy name.

Christalla's testimony illustrates how God has moved mightily in one particular place; Ffald-y-Brenin. This place is undeniably special, it is a Holy site. Christalla and I simply love the place.

However, we do not advocate the elevation of the channel or the means above the Lord Himself.

God's redemptive power is clearly at work in specific locations throughout the world, where He works special miracles. Why in these particular places? Because He has created things through which He wants to reveal Himself to us. God will use whoever and whatever He desires to fulfil His will and purpose.

When Christalla and I share our testimonies about the miraculous things that take place at Ffald-y-Brenin, we encourage others to look past the physical aspect of the retreat itself and to the reality of God.

Some people that Christalla and I have met at Ffald-y-Brenin, talked about the absence of miracles and healings taking place in their places of worship.

They spoke about a corporate leaning towards cessationism, the theology that the miraculous gifts of the Holy Spirit such as speaking in tongues, prophetic utterances and healing, ceased to occur outside of the New Testament era.

Others told us that although their fellow Christians believe that present day miracles do take place, they only happen in special circumstances and usually to other people; therefore they don't happen that often.

So, when they heard about a place where God was demonstrating His divine power, they wanted to meet with Him there. They wanted to experience His presence and spread the good news that the Holy Spirit is still doing incredible things and by the grace of God take His anointing back to their churches.

Our Lord is able to heal a person anyplace, anywhere, anytime and Christalla and I have seen this happen, many times. God is omnipotent (all powerful) and omnipresent (everywhere at the same time). Despite this, we still visit Ffald-y-Brenin, as others will do to other sites where there are manifestations of God's miracles because of the expectation that He will continue to act.

Where is Your Faith? – Just Believe!

2

Brian Smitheram

It was during a Sunday morning service at my church – the City Temple – that I first heard Brian's testimony. Our Pastor, Steve Ball, invited Brian to join him on the podium to share his personal experience of God's healing power with the congregation. Brian's warm West Country accent seemed to deepen the poignancy of his words which were deeply moving.

Following the service I decided to approach Brian and ask if he would allow me to feature his testimony in this book.

I introduced myself to Brian and said, 'I want to write about the testimonies of people in this church. I want to tell others, both Christians and non-believers, about how real the Lord is to us today, how He is working miracles in our lives.'

Brian fixed me with a steady gaze and said, 'You already know the answer to that question, of course I will. Why wouldn't I want everyone to know about the healing power of our Lord?'

Here is Brian's account of how God healed him:

It was January 13, 2006. I was at a birthday party with friends but was also celebrating the birth of our eighth child who had been born a few days earlier on January 5. The raising of my eyebrows prompted Brian to say, 'Yes, I did say it was our eighth child, my wife and I like children.'

The following Saturday morning I lost consciousness as I was walking upstairs. I fell backwards from the ninth step, head first, all the way back down the stairs.

When I regained consciousness I realised I was lying in a pool of my own blood. It came from my nose which had hit the post at the bottom of the stairs. My neck was pushed up against a book case and the rest of my body lay on the stairs.

I asked my wife to help me move my legs as I couldn't feel them. She said she had rung the emergency services and had been told by a doctor not to move me.

The medics arrived and I was taken to hospital. Following several tests and scans, a consultant came to see me. The first words he uttered were, 'Well…I am very impressed.'

I asked him why he was impressed. He told me he had made this assertion because I was still alive. He said that I should have died because of my injuries. He told me that I had broken my neck in two places and that I had also fractured my back.

So, as a consequence of the damage that had been done to my body I would never walk again. Then just to make sure I had gotten the message he stated that if I had my leg amputated today, I would still be able to feel my foot itch.

I had broken the C1 and C2 vertebrae which are the first and second bones in my neck and as a result of this, the nerves in my neck were in bad shape. This meant that I would be unable to feel anything from the neck downwards. He said that even if my neck had escaped injury the break in my back would have done the same job, so I would have to get used to life in a wheelchair because there was no hope of me ever walking ever again.

So there you have it.

I was strapped to a bed and unable to move. It took six people to lift me, just so I could use a bed pan. That didn't go down well with me, there are just some things in life that you need to do for yourself. What was I going to tell my wife?

'Well, dear, you now have nine children to look after.'

'It will be okay dear; they are going to fit me to some wheels soon so I can be half man and half car.'

'Now the insurance company will be paying you for a change.'

I felt the Holy Spirit say to me, 'Don't worry.' I had a peace in my spirit, so I didn't receive what the doctor told me, I kept on trusting God's word.

I remained strapped to the bed. Two days later I was going to be taken to the operating theatre and fitted with a halo brace and a back brace.

It was a Monday morning. As I was being pushed to theatre I caught a glimpse of someone in a metal cage, he looked like somebody had crossed him between Metal Micky and Robo-Cop. Little did I know what lay in store for me.

What a fun day that turned out to be! Lying on a table with a guy looking down at me with an electric drill in his hand.

'What are you going to do with that?' I asked.

'I am going to drill some bolts into the front and back of your head,' was his reply.

'Wow…so you are going to do this while I am still awake?'

'Yes,' he retorted in a matter of fact sort of way. (At that point if I could have got myself off that table I would have!)

'It's okay,' he said, 'you won't feel it as your nerves have died by now and it's only your brain telling you it might hurt.'

That was easy for him to say, he was not the one lying on the table.

'No need to worry and besides, if you close your eyes you won't see the drill going into your skull – it's just the noise of the drill that makes you think it is going to hurt. I have done this countless times before and I can promise you that won't feel the drill digging into your flesh and bone.'

If you feel sick at this point in the story, what do you think I was feeling like?

Sure as eggs are eggs he put the first bolt in my forehead and I didn't feel a thing. The second one was a different matter though. As soon as the bolt started to dig into my skin, I felt terrible pain. They put me to sleep to complete the drilling.

When I woke up everything was done but what they didn't know at the time was that the bolt had gone into a nerve and that the nerve was still alive. (That bolt caused me so much pain, that within a few weeks of leaving the hospital, I had to go back and have a second operation to get it removed and have a new one put in.)

On Tuesday morning I was in tremendous pain. My back hurt, my head hurt, my neck hurt, there was not a place in my body that was not in pain. My nurse told me that there was a distinct possibility that I would die from my injuries.

I was given liquid morphine to ease the pain. This was administered every hour, throughout the day and night.

To my horror the morphine had absolutely no effect! I felt as if I was going to die and there was nothing I or any of the hospital staff could do.

It was now Wednesday and somehow I was still alive. An X-ray was arranged for me to ensure that the halo and back brace were fitted correctly, so that the broken bones would have the best possible chance to heal. After the X-ray was taken they checked it against the one taken on Saturday.

There was a major problem...the two X-rays didn't match!

The patient was the right person, the hospital number was correct, but the X-ray was showing no broken bones in my back. Thank You Lord!

Saturday's X-ray showed a clear break in my back, and the one taken on Wednesday showed that the fissure had fused together and mended. It was strange that this should happen because it is impossible for broken bones to heal within four days.

I believe that it was God at work in my body. Three more days passed and on the Saturday morning some doctors came to see me. They told me I could try to get out of bed and maybe take a few steps.

A couple of nurses got a dressing gown for me and helped me out of the bed. As I put my weight on my feet a doctor said, 'Try to walk a few steps please.' I was just about to try and move but started to fall forward. The doctors caught me.

'Now you know you will never walk again,' said one of the doctors.

I asked the doctors for permission to leave the ward to go outside to get some fresh air. I needed to get my head around everything that was happening to me. I was told that I could try if I wanted to.

I rang my wife and asked her to bring in a wheelchair we had at home, so I could try to move around a little. This she did for the next few days and I was able to get on and off the ward with the help of the nurses.

On Monday, I was sitting in the chair outside the concourse of the hospital and I started to talk to God. It came to my mind that if God was who He said He was, and that He was able to do what He said He can do, then why was I sitting in a wheelchair? If I believed what the bible said, that all things are possible if we have faith the size of a mustard seed and that this small amount of faith could move a mountain, well this was some mountain for me and I needed it moved. I took hold of the Word and decided to try and stand.

I was able to get myself onto a bench. I dragged the wheelchair in front of me and declared that if God was for me then nothing would stand in my way.

Then something truly amazing happened. With the aid of the wheelchair I was doing it...I was walking! Wow! Thank you Lord. I thought of Psalm 91. His word was true.

When I walked onto the ward the nurses were livid because if I had fallen and landed on any of the bolts which were inserted in the front or the back of my head, then they would have gone straight into my brain and that would have finished me off.

By the twelfth day the hospital decided to send me home because I would not stay in bed. For someone to break their neck and back and walk out of hospital within twelve days can only be because of God and the miracles only He can do.

I still had to stay in the halo and back brace for a further four months and that was hard for me. Trying to move around and not being able to bend or turn took a lot of getting used to. It also took its toll on my family and especially my wife, as she had to look after all the children plus a new born baby. This was a very difficult time for us, but with God's grace and the help of many friends in the church, we were able to move forward and grow in Christ.

When I look back now I can see where God gave me four to five miracles in just a few short days. Also, I know the doctors still can't believe that I am walking again because the medical profession deemed it to be impossible. However, if you put your trust in Jesus Christ and believe with all your heart that He is the Lord of Lords and the King of Kings, God's own Son, then you too will see the impossible happen in your life.

The majority of people who suffer the same type of accident as I did will have metal plates in their neck or some kind of scaffolding/metal bars to support it.

I tell you the truth. God has fully restored my neck and back. There are no metal plates or bars in my neck, just complete healing as the word of God says in the bible.

What a Saviour we have, bless His Holy name!

'Because he holds fast to me in love, I will deliver him; I will protect him, because he knows my name. When he calls to me, I will answer him; I will be with him in trouble; I will rescue him,' (Psalm 91:14-15).

Where is Your Faith? – Just Believe!

3

Denise Thomson

Denise met Christalla several years ago through a charitable organisation called M.E. Support in Glamorgan (MESiG). At that time Denise was suffering with Myalgic Encephalomyelitis (M.E.), as was Christalla. The two women immediately connected and have since become the best of friends. Christalla and I both cherish Denise's friendship. She has such a loving nature and loves the Lord with all her heart.

This is her story:

In 1999 I was living in a privately rented flat in London. I was a single mother with two small children and had a very hectic lifestyle. During that year I suffered a severe bout of flu from which I never fully recovered. Given my commitments, I simply didn't have enough time to recuperate. I was continually ill with colds, sore throats and tonsillitis.

This was not a good time in my life to be told that my tenancy contract was not going to be renewed. I spiralled into a blind panic. The Local Housing Authority advised me to declare myself homeless which would have qualified me for shared housing, but that option would have been inappropriate for my children. My parents suggested moving back home with them but I fought that with every sinew. That would never have worked out, believe me.

Where is Your Faith? – Just Believe!

I eventually found a squalid little flat on the North Circular road. It was the unhealthiest environment imaginable. The traffic fumes were disgusting and there was raw sewage seeping from a broken pipe that ran alongside the bottom of the stairwell. There was no heating on my floor which meant that the flat was freezing, and the roof leaked. If I ran a bath the water became cold in a very short period of time.

So, my daughter and I would boil kettles of water to pour into the bath, just so it was warm enough to get into. To compound matters further there was a nail bar shop downstairs and a cleaning business next door, which meant that we were constantly inhaling noxious chemicals. My body couldn't cope with this incessant bombardment. Sometimes I was so poorly that I reluctantly had to ask my nine year old daughter to take her younger brother to school.

I decided to enrol in college to retrain but was hampered by the steady deterioration in my health. I had the intellect to study in higher education but felt as if I was dyslexic. One day I collapsed in college and couldn't walk. My tutors were mortified, given that I only had three remaining weeks to complete my studies. They tried their best to support me but I was too ill to continue and had to drop out of college.

On the May 8, 2001, my brother-in-law died. He had been suffering with epilepsy. A day later...I was diagnosed with M.E.

I saw a number of doctors who clearly did not know what they were dealing with. One doctor told me to go home and take a paracetamol.

I researched the illness via the internet and discovered that M.E. related to the inflammation of the brain but apart from that there was very little information to be had. I proceeded to have every blood test imaginable but all the returns were clear.

During this time I met someone called Sean from Cardiff. He was very supportive of me and tried to understand my condition. Things developed between us and he asked me to move in with him. I was really grateful for the opportunity to leave my flat but given that his home was built on a hill, it was very tiring for me to walk anywhere in the vicinity of his house. Sean later decided to move back to Cardiff and I followed with the children.

We rented a house together and tried to live as normally as possible. However, our relationship suffered as Sean increasingly struggled to cope with my illness and we eventually separated.

As time went on I went through a process of thinking that I was improving because I would have periods when I felt full of energy and would be able to function at a higher level. Sadly, these periods of semi-normality became less frequent and I could only manage to leave the house on a once, or twice weekly basis.

I tried a number of self-help courses which proved to be in-effective. I became almost totally housebound.

I came across a support group called for people who suffered with M.E. / Fibromyalgia and in the process of doing so met Christalla, aka Chris, who became a dear friend to me.

In 2009 I developed a chest infection which my doctor was unable to treat because the prescribed medication was ineffective. I was in despair. I was sleeping for eighteen hours per day, sometimes more. I couldn't feed myself so I lived off muffins and had a kettle by my bedside which enabled me to make myself cups of tea. I didn't have a stair lift so was trapped upstairs in my home. My children tried to help me as much as they could but they had their own lives to live. I was thankful that they were invited to friends' houses for meals and sleep-overs, it gave them some normality.

In October 2011, I heard that Christalla had been miraculously healed at a Christian retreat called Ffald-y-Brenin. We spoke on the phone and she arranged to visit me. She told me that she would be accompanied by our mutual friend, Linda.

When Christalla arrived she could hardly contain her excitement as she eagerly told me that she had received a prophetic word from God. She said, 'He told me that you're the next to be healed at Ffald-y-Brenin. I was first now it's your turn.'

I told her that there was absolutely no possibility of me travelling to a place which was two hours away. Also, I was unable to sit upright for long periods and had great difficulty in opening my eyes. Chris and Linda tried their best to persuade me to try to make the journey but I flatly refused to comply.

Christalla and Linda offered to take me to the 'Healing Rooms' at the Woodville Church in Cardiff. I loved going there to meet with God.

On the days when ministry took place all the chairs used for Sunday worship were stored away. Mats, blankets and pillows were then placed on the floor where individuals could lie down and relax whilst listening to soft worship music. Each person would then be joined by one or sometimes two members of the prayer team, who would ask the individual what they wanted God to do for them.

Following our arrival I couldn't wait to enter God's presence. I lay down, covered myself with a blanket and closed my eyes. Bliss!

The person who came to administer prayer asked what I would like the Lord to do for me. 'Um…to be brave enough to travel to Ffald-y-Brenin,' I said. I didn't believe for one minute that this might actually happen.

Then something incredible occurred! I felt the spirit of fear lift off me. I was filled with joy and ran around the room telling people that I was going to travel to Ffald-y-Brenin. Most people in the room who had heard the story of Christalla's miraculous healing said they would pray that the same thing would happen to me.

Chris and Linda heard me making a commotion and had to ask someone what was going on. Poor things, after all their efforts they were the last to know about my change of heart.

Arrangements were made for me to travel with Chris and Ken to attend the upcoming prayer day at Ffald-y-Brenin. I was forewarned that it was going to be an early start for the two hour journey. I must admit that the thought of travelling for that length of time did concern me, but I prayed against my fear.

It had taken a huge effort to get myself ready to travel at seven o'clock in the morning. I would usually be fast asleep at this time of the day. I heard a knock on the door I assumed was Ken. I grabbed my cane and slowly made my way through the hall towards the door. As I did so I glimpsed my image in the mirror. Oh dear! I was ashen and my eyes were partially open. As I opened the door I had to almost completely shut my eyes to ease the pain caused by the natural light.

When we arrived at Christalla's house we were met by some friends who had arranged to travel with us in separate cars. Christalla led the prayer with an expectancy that great things were going to happen that day.

During most of the journey to Ffald-y-Brenin I drifted in and out of consciousness whilst being uplifted by God's love through the lyrics of worship songs being played in the front of the car.

I remember at one point being woken by the slowing momentum of the car which I sensed was an indication of us drawing nearer to our destination.

Whilst journeying through the countryside of West Wales my spirit was lifted by the breath-taking beauty of God's creation.

When we arrived at the chapel in Cwm Gwaun village, I was relieved that we had finally arrived because I was exhausted and ached all over. My body felt twice its biological age as I slowly stepped out of our vehicle.

Ken gathered my bedding to take it into the chapel because I knew I would not be able to sit upright for very long. Chris walked beside me as aided by my black cane I limped towards the entrance of the chapel.

Once inside the chapel we were greeted by two women who Chris introduced as Hilary and Hazel. They were members of the Ffald-y-Brenin team. I was struck by the compassion in their eyes as Chris told them how poorly I was. I was grateful that they were so accommodating in finding a place for me to set up a makeshift bed, despite the lack of space available.

My first attempt at sitting on a chair lasted around fifteen minutes and then I had to go and lie down. I felt so ill and was so cold that I couldn't stop shivering. I made two unsuccessful attempts to sit on my chair again, then gave up, I just wasn't well enough. Christalla and Ken gathered some coats from some kind souls and piled them on top of me. I felt much warmer and slowly closed my eyes.

I recall Christalla coming over to sit with me and I said, 'I just want God to tell me if he wants me to live or die. I don't mind which one it is, I just need to know.'

I had reached a point of utter desperation. She said, 'What you are feeling right now, is not of God, He doesn't want you to die. I know because He told me that you are going to be healed.'

I was so grateful to hear those words and immediately sensed the hope rising in me.

At the end of the service Roy made the announcement that a session of healing ministry would shortly be taking place. I went and sat next to Chris and Ken for a little while before joining the long queue that stretched almost the entire length of the building. Given the large numbers of people seeking ministry Roy asked several members of his team to assist.

When I heard this I became dismayed because I had my heart set on Roy and his wife Daphne ministering to me. I said a prayer asking God if He would make that happen for me. As I approached the head of the queue Daphne suddenly came over to me and said, 'I don't know why, but I sense that you need to be ministered to by Roy and myself, don't go to anyone else.'

A huge wave of relief swept over me. God had shown me that He was with me. I sensed that something extraordinary was going to happen. My turn for ministry came. As I stepped forward I could feel my heart pounding.

Roy asked me some questions about my condition and put his right palm on my forehead. I felt something surge through me and felt as if I wanted to sink to the floor. I felt Daphne's arm around my waist but knew that she would struggle to support my weight if I went to ground. I got an apology in quickly by saying, 'I'm a big girl, it might be a struggle.' I recall someone coming up behind me and gently touching my back. The person was indicating that it was safe to allow myself to fall if I so wished. I was relieved because I couldn't have stood up much longer. I handed everything over to God...then everything went blank.

When I regained consciousness I was helped to my feet by Ken and Daphne. Then Roy spoke a blessing over me. When Roy had finished speaking I began to look for my cane. Roy said, 'You won't be needing that anymore, take Ken's arm if you feel unsteady on your feet. Don't worry you will be fine.'

I did as Roy instructed and held onto Ken's arm as we made our way towards the exit. But praise God, by the time I got to the door my strength returned and I strode confidently out of the building. I was healed!

We drove up to the Ffald-y-Brenin Christian retreat which is about two miles from Cwm Gwaun village. As I got out of the car I felt full of energy. We walked from the car park to the little chapel and then along the bridal path to the high cross. I was so jubilant that I just wanted to run and run through the fields below us. I stretched out my arms in front of the cross and thanked God for healing me.

Prior to returning to Cardiff a number of us went into the craft room which has a stunning view of the valley. Whilst we were relaxing with our cups of tea and coffee, Ken shouted, 'Look everyone, look at Denise's face!' I was told that my eyes were bright and my skin was glowing. Apparently I looked as if I had just had a sun bathing session. Someone said that the light of God was shining out from within me.

My full recovery took several months to come to fruition. During this time the enemy attempted to trick me into accepting the lie that my illness had not left me. However, I never stopped believing that God had healed me. He had been true to the word that He had given Chris that said I would be healed. She gave me a lot of support to ensure that I was vigilant in recognising and countering those attacks of the enemy. This helped me to stand in the faithfulness and truth of the Word of God.

I think it is important to state that although my healing took place at Ffald-y-Brenin God can, and does, heal anytime, anywhere. His thoughts are above our thoughts and His ways are not like ours (Isaiah 55:8). When He chose to rescue me, He did it according to his plans and purposes.

'I know the plans I have for you, declares the Lord. Plans to prosper you and not to harm you, plans to give you hope and a future,' (Jeremiah 29:11).

4

James

*Given the sensitive nature of the work that James has to
undertake in his professional capacity, his surname
has been omitted to protect his identity.*

It was a cold evening in February 2011. I remember the eager anticipation that Christalla and I felt as we took our seats to watch our first baptismal service at the City Temple church.

Each person to be baptised gave an account to the congregation of how they came to Lord. We heard some amazing and moving stories. I was struck in particular, however, by the testimony of a tall young man. He couldn't contain his excitement about getting baptised and eulogised about what his saviour had done for him. He spoke with such passion and conviction...it was simply awe inspiring. As he was about to be submerged into the baptismal waters he punched the air with unbridled joy and exclaimed loudly, 'I love You, Jesus.'

A few weeks later I was introduced to James. He was tall man with a shock of curly brown hair. As his hand grasped mine, I found myself looking into his bespectacled eyes which shone brightly. The light of the Lord was clearly within him.

'The eyes are like a lamp for the body. If your eyes are sound, your whole body will be full of light,' (Matthew 6:22).

'I would love to contribute to your book,' he said. 'Just let me know when and where.'

A few weeks later I met James on a cold December afternoon at his favourite coffee shop, an establishment that was renowned for its delicious 'healthy' cakes. I decided to forgo the cakes until later but ordered coffee for us both and settled into my chair with an air of eager anticipation.

James set the context of our meeting with a prayer which was conducted without fear or embarrassment of others who were clearly able to hear what he was saying. That was a truly powerful moment.

At the end of the prayer we talked excitedly about what God was doing in our lives. I listened intently, enthralled by his sheer unbridled love for Jesus. Each sentence he uttered was punctuated with praise for the Lord. We became so engrossed in our conversation I almost forgot that I needed to interview him about his testimony.

James has a deep passion for the Lord which is just awe inspiring, it truly is. Since meeting James he has become a dear friend to Christalla and I. We simply love the guy.

Here is his story:

I was born and brought up in South Wales and enjoyed my childhood immensely. I had several siblings which caused my parents to feel overwhelmed at times, so my grandparents stepped in and helped out by bringing me up.

James told me without any hint of arrogance that as a child he had been very popular and had a good heart.

I would help anyone and would often assist the elderly in my village with shopping and chores. I couldn't understand why none of my peers did anything like this. I struggled with lessons at school. I found it difficult to concentrate and my memory retention was poor. I compensated for this with quick wit and humour but gained a reputation at school for being disruptive during class. As a consequence I left mainstream education without formal qualifications.

It wasn't until James was twenty seven years of age that he was diagnosed as having dyslexia.

At the age of seventeen I attended college for further education whilst still living with my grandparents. There was a lot of love in the house, lots of children were always there. My Nan would give anything she had to anyone. This experience enriched me and gave me a desire to work with young people.

At this stage of my life I developed a love for horses and became a skilled show jumper winning several competitions. I gained a Childcare and Education qualification at college and found a placement working with young children.

I saw a poster in college advertising an exchange programme through an organisation called *Camp America*. This was the kind of work I had always wanted to do. Camp America matched students with their counterparts in the US, all of whom were keen to become involved in specific projects that would benefit the community.

I was chosen to work with underprivileged children in a camp based in upstate New York. The benefactor of the camp was the famous singer Mariah Carey. I met her on one occasion when she made an impromptu visit to see the kids.

The project was a career awareness programme with the emphasis on sharpening the aspiration and goals of young people. There was a focus on breaking the pattern of the route these kids would take into the drug/rapper culture.

I returned to Wales but with a view to going back to the US as soon as the opportunity presented itself. Upon my return home though, things began to go awry. I was a risk taker, I would do anything for a dare, and I would stick up for anyone in the community, with no thought for myself. I was the joker who made everyone laugh.

As a consequence of being so well liked, my friends and associates elevated me to a status that I did not aspire to. I reluctantly became their leader, someone to look up to.

It was around this time that I started to develop a desire for other men. I would go out with my heterosexual friends and prior to the end of the evening would pretend that I was tired, say my goodbyes and then would head off to the gay clubs. I began to experiment with illegal substances in these clubs. I would get absolutely 'stewed off my face on drugs' because I was so fearful of someone I knew seeing me entering these establishments. I was embarking on a path that led to one destination – destruction.

Whilst I was frequenting gay clubs I entered a world of complete darkness. I found myself in all sorts of situations with different men. I became involved in same sex relationships and within two of those relationships I became the victim of domestic violence. One person treated me so abominably that I increased my drug usage in an attempt to alleviate the constant rejection.

I took out bank loans and 'maxed' my credit card to buy expensive clothes, drugs and cars. I was trying to buy myself into a good career, I wanted social significance. I was trying to buy confidence. I contemplated making adjustments to my body and even considered a facelift. Just to be accepted in the gay scene you had to have a certain physique, be a certain type of person and modify your God given gifts. It was crazy!

Romans 1:25-27 and 1 Timothy 1:8-10 are scriptures that give clear instructions about how we are to conduct our lives.

James

Homosexuality (romantic and sexualised behaviour between members of the same sex) is strictly forbidden. However, it is important to understand that God does not hate gay people because He is love. He just abhors the sin. Nothing a person does can make God love them anymore or any less. He loves everyone unconditionally.

Everyone around me thought I was doing really well. The kind of remarks being made were, 'James is always going away on holiday, he's off to America again, he's really successful.'

The reality was that I was crumbling. I was spending large amounts of money because of the overflow of my grief and sadness. Much of this happened because I never really had a father when I was growing up. I never really had a secure, masculine attachment. I just wanted to be loved. I was looking for love in men just to feel significant...to feel wanted.

I attempted to fill my emotional void by increasing my drug usage. I took drugs at different times for different reasons but initially it was to increase my confidence. I felt a certain kind of pressure to maintain my standing amongst my peers.

As time progressed I formed relationships with individuals who were at a hard-core level in terms of drug taking. My life changed dramatically for the worse and I descended into darkness for two years.

James' voice softened and was clearly tinged with sadness as he continued to share his experiences with me.

I began to take drugs in my grandmother's house without her knowledge. I had rest periods from using substances but unfortunately these sabbaticals were soon followed by drug taking binge sessions which compensated for the time I spent in abstention.

Where is Your Faith? – Just Believe!

Members of my family looked up to me, however, this status brought responsibility with it. I was expected to find solutions for family problems. I became the principal carer for my grandfather who, when his health deteriorated, had his leg amputated. I counselled my alcoholic uncle and one day found him dead, he had hung himself. My mother and father cut him down and I thought I could see his chest moving so I tried to ring for an ambulance. I tried several times but couldn't get a signal on my mobile. I was devastated.

Two months after the death of my uncle a close family friend doused herself with petrol and burned herself to death.

As a consequence of the trauma of my uncle dying I developed panic attacks and paranoia. I became scared of my own shadow. When I arrived home, I would cover my eyes with my hand as I entered the house and would feel for the light switch because I was petrified of seeing a manifestation of my uncle. I would turn every light on in the house and sing at the top of my voice to break the silence barrier. I was frightened of the possibility of even hearing a pin drop. In hindsight this was partly to do with the fresh memory of my uncle passing away but mostly caused by my drug dependency.

I tried everything humanly possible to break my addiction; doctors, specialist health care, anti-depressants and counselling but my drug addiction escalated and I started to use cocaine and heroin. To compound matters further, my maternal and paternal grandfathers died within two days of each other. At that point in time I lost total control of my life. I recall my mother looking into my eyes and saying, 'Son, the light has gone out.'

I took fifteen drug overdoses within a two year period. I found myself in all sorts of places, even the gutter. I failed my university course and lost my work placement because my written work was substandard. At home my grandmother even stopped taking cups of tea to my room for fear of finding me dead. I was admitted to hospital several times and amazed the medical staff by my longevity. I recall lying on a hospital bed when a nurse told me that my heart was beating so fast I was running the equivalent of a marathon. She told me that I should be dead. 'I don't know what's keeping you alive,' she said.

As James related these experiences I found it hard to believe that the man sat in front of me had previously been so broken and desperate.

I had previously visited Greece and bought a small wooden cross which I brought home with me and kept in my bedroom. I recall how I used to cling to the cross during my worst periods of drug abuse whilst sobbing in desperation. Sometimes I couldn't even cry because the drugs had dried up my tear ducts.

I felt so alone. I would say to God, 'If you were real, you wouldn't allow this to happen to me.'

A couple of months later I took a massive overdose of drugs. However, this time something was very different. I sensed darkness enveloping me and felt as if he was walking towards my death bed. I could feel myself slipping away and heard an audible voice say, 'James get up, you have (finally) done it.' I quickly put on my dressing gown, flung open the door and sprinted down the road towards my mother's house.

When I arrived I was hysterical. 'Ring for an ambulance mum...quickly please!' I shouted. She tried to calm me down because she had seen me in this situation many times previously.

'Let's talk this through,' she said.

I pleaded with her to make the phone call because I knew without any doubt that I was dying. I was rolling on the floor and didn't have the energy to get to my feet. I couldn't get up. It was as if the life had been sucked out of me. There was no way back, the wheels of the plane had been retracted, the engines of the plane had been cut, the plane was coming in to land. Finally, in exasperation I made the call myself.

The ambulance arrived and conveyed me to hospital. Once there I slipped into unconsciousness. My mother later told me that my body went into a drug induced anaphylactic shock which is akin to an epileptic fit. She said that a team of medics desperately tried to resuscitate me but I wasn't responding.

I had no awareness of what the medics were doing but it felt as if my spirit was leaving the earth. I knew that I was having an out of body experience because I'd had them previously during heavy drug taking episodes. This time, however, it was different.

I felt compelled to give my sister some final words of advice because I sensed in my spirit that I was dying. As I did so, something incredible happened. I saw the coast of Africa. I could see the lights defining the shape of the continent as I was floating upwards. Shortly after that everything went black.

James truly believed that he had died that night.

Three days later I opened my eyes. I was in a hospital bed. The curtains opened and in walked a man with a kind face. He introduced himself and told me that he was a doctor. As he examined me I was struck by his kindness and consideration. This was unlike the majority of his colleagues who had quite understandably become exasperated with me, given the frequency of my visits to the Accident and Emergency unit.

James told me that during the conversation with the doctor it transpired that the gentleman was from Israel. This wasn't particularly significant at the time but would eventually become a major facet of his walk with God.

The doctor said, 'You are going to be alright.' I felt refreshed as if my life had been given back to me. I knew something was different and I was determined to change.

About a week later I went to Greece for a few days to recuperate. I found a small church near to where I was staying which always seemed to be empty. I would go there every day, lie on the floor and beg God for help. The day before I left for home I heard a voice in my heart clearly say, 'Go to church, go to the City Temple.

When I returned home I did as the Lord instructed me and began to attend the City Temple church. I remember going there on a Sunday night with a friend and sitting in the upper tiers. There was an altar call for people who wanted prayer. You should have seen me – my feet didn't touch the floor! I literally flew down the steps. I was so desperate to be covered in prayer...for someone to help me.

During subsequent weeks I participated in the *Alpha* course but was still ambivalent about what God could do in my life. I was doubtful because the drug addiction was like a cancer, it affected every aspect of my life. I continued to attend the City Temple because the people there really cared for me and I loved the ambience of the place, which on reflection was clearly the presence of the Lord.

A few weeks later the City Temple organised a 'Holy Spirit Day' at the Beacon Centre, which is an affiliated church in another part of Cardiff. During the service my friend encouraged me to walk to the altar with her and once we were there she said, 'Do you want to give your life to the Lord?' Without hesitation I said, 'Yes.'

She prayed over me and gently led me to the Lord. I closed my eyes and suddenly felt as if I had been plugged into an electric pylon; the energy was so powerful. I felt as if the drug addiction was being shaken out of me. I knew that God was real from that point onwards. I walked away from that altar completely renewed, a brand new creation.

My family and friends could not believe the transformation. I was and still am a walking multi-miracle. Since that day everything has changed. The Lord's redemptive power has delivered me from homosexuality and my addiction to illegal substances, prescribed drugs and alcohol. He healed my depression, emotional pain, anxiety disorder, loneliness, fear, and rejection. He washed away my guilt and the bitterness I felt towards myself, for the damage that I had caused my family.

I see my life as a new minted coin that through the years had become grubby and tarnished. It has been flicked up to heaven into Jesus' hands, lovingly polished and made to look like new again. *'For I will restore you to health and I will heal you of your wounds,'* (Jeremiah 30:17). Praise God!

5

Leonie Riley

At the time of writing this story Leonie and her husband Tim were the worship team leaders at the Cardiff City Temple church. Leonie was the lead singer of the team and has the most beautiful voice. Leonie blessed Christalla and I by decorating the City Temple church for our wedding and also by singing for us during the ceremony. Tim contributed by playing the piano and by singing with his wife. Christalla and I are indebted to them both for helping to make our big day such a success.

Here is Leonie's amazing testimony:

When I was a little girl I knew about the Lord and as soon as I was old enough to be allowed out on my own to play I used to go to the Salvation Army church. How amazing is that! When I was thirteen I gave my life to the Lord.

As soon as I was fifteen I went off and did my own thing and by the time is was twenty three I had given birth to my daughter Ruby. At that point in my life I had tried everything; alcohol, drugs, self-help techniques and Taoism. You name it I tried it. When I practiced transcendental meditation I had a number of out of body experiences. During this period in my life I suffered many drug overdoses, suicidal depression, bi-polar disorder, psychosis and anxiety induced psychosis. All this took place between the ages of fifteen and thirty three which is the age I was when I was living near London with a partner. I left him because of abuse issues which involved my daughter and returned to Cardiff.

It wasn't long after my return to Cardiff that I made a massive suicide attempt by using alcohol, illegal substances and prescriptive drugs. I was in a crack (drug) den with my daughter Ruby at the time. She realised that I was dying and raised the alarm. Ruby was ten years old.

When the paramedics arrived I was quickly taken into the ambulance so they could undertake procedures to try and save my life. Ruby was terrified and looked so vulnerable. This stirred my heart and I cried out, 'What have I done, God help me!' Then as clear as day I heard the words, 'Call upon the Lord and you will be saved.'

I turned to see who had spoken and saw two paramedics, one of whom was taking notes and the other unsuccessfully trying to insert an intravenous line into my vein, which had started to collapse. I quickly realised that the voice hadn't come from either of them, so I screamed again, 'God, save me!'

And then the same voice said, 'Not God...Jesus...call upon the name of the Lord Jesus Christ and you will be saved.' So with all the strength left in me I screamed out, 'Jesus!'

I then had an out of body experience where I saw myself lying on the stretcher in the ambulance. When they took me to the hospital I was unconscious but could see that the nurses were panic stricken and remember wondering why they were acting in that manner.

A while after this I had a vision where the Lord showed me that when I was crying out, He was stood right in front of me. The words of the audible voice are quoted in Scripture in Acts 2:21, *'Whoever calls upon the name of the Lord shall be saved.'*

God could have healed me there and then of course but I believe that He was showing me that His promises in the Bible are true, that we can stand in His word.

Three days later I woke up on the Toxins ward of the Heath Hospital in Cardiff. A doctor sat on the end of the bed. I squeezed his hand and asked, 'Am I dead?' He said, 'No, but we have no idea how you are still alive.'

I recall tests being done and that there was fixed dilation in the pupil of my left eye. In my right eye there were only minute reflexes. I felt trapped in my body and was desperate to move but couldn't. The doctors were at a complete loss of what to do, they were powerless to help me.

Whilst I was in the hospital I regularly lapsed in and out of consciousness. I remember waking one night and through the window I could see a really bright star. At that moment I felt as if I had never taken a drug or a drink in my entire life.

When I was well enough to leave hospital I received psychological and psychiatric treatment. It took nine months to be healed of my bad memories and suicidal tendencies.

During this period my daughter and I went to live in a women's refuge. I remember on one particular night praying and asking in that prayer, 'Why can't I die? Why after all the suicide attempts am I still here? Why am I being saved?' I was desperate to get off this planet.

I would take my daughter to school wearing my pyjamas under my clothes then I would go back to the refuge and lie on my bed. Life didn't seem worth living. Sometimes I would be aware of hot tears rolling down my face but it didn't feel as if I was sobbing. Before I knew it I would be crying and praying, I would say, 'God, you must be there…you must be there.'

Where is Your Faith? – Just Believe!

After nine months my daughter and I were re-housed. At that time I was abusing alcohol heavily. A friend of mine, who I had regained contact with when I returned to Cardiff, copied some CDs for me. I was drawn to one particular track called *Jesus Take the Wheel* by Carrie Underwood.

Jesus take the wheel; take it from my hand, cause I can't do this on my own; I'm letting go...so give me one more chance, save me from this road I'm on....Jesus take the wheel.

I played it morning, noon and night. One day, Ruby came home from school and said in exasperation, 'Mummy, please don't put the Jesus song on again, why are you playing it?'

That night and at the beginning of the next day I repeatedly questioned myself. I would ask, 'Why am I playing this song?'

I can't remember exactly if it was the first glass of my second bottle or the second glass of my first bottle but I had consumed a lot of cider by 11.30am of the following morning.

I asked myself the 'why am I playing this?' question again, then began to sing the song out loud. I leaned against the worktop in the kitchen looked up to the sky and felt the inspiration to tip the rest of the cider into the sink...which I did.

A couple of days later I was in my bedroom using the vacuum cleaner when the words *'I am the way, the truth and the life'* suddenly came to me. I'd obviously remembered those words from Sunday school at the Salvation Army.

I immediately stopped what I was doing and with every ounce of energy I could muster I shouted, 'Okay! You said you are truth. If all the thirty three years of my life have been a lie, which they have, you show me truth.'

Within two weeks I'd met Hayley Byfield and Peter Ackerman who at that time were both members of the City Temple church.

They have both since gone on to do amazing things for God. Hayley was the one who led me back to Jesus.

I attended the City Temple on the first Sunday of October 2007 and apparently Tim, who is now my husband, came to the service for the first time on exactly the same day! We didn't know each other at the time. Isn't that amazing?

There was a song playing, *Worthy is the Lamb,* which talks about 'the darling of heaven crucified.' Seeing those words in front of me on the screen then and even now, is so incredible. Jesus is the darling of heaven and He died for me! In my mind's eye I could see His head bowed with a crown of thorns on it and I just started to shake and cry and said, 'I'm sorry.' It was time to admit my responsibility. I wasn't completely in the wrong but I had done a lot of things to myself and needed to be accountable for that.

I received a revelation of what the crucifixion and resurrection was all about, it all made sense to me. The truth had got hold of me when Hayley and Pete had witnessed to me. It was going off in me like a rocket but the truth of the resurrection and the fact that the Lord is coming back knocked me the right side up.

The only way to accurately describe it is this way; I had been walking backwards and on my head for thirty three years, now I was the right side up and it felt great. I didn't miss a Sunday service during that time and don't think I have since. I was born again. I loved the Lord and craved the word of God.

About a year later I began to get chest pains and became constantly fatigued. Regardless of this I was on fire for the Lord. There was no stopping this girl! You know when you get a new plant and then the roots sprout out all over the place? Well, I was like this new budding plant, I was just flying with God. It didn't matter what was in store I knew Jesus was going to carry me through everything.

Around this period in my life we had new neighbours move in next door and things quickly became pretty desperate for me and my daughter. The noise and environmental pollution that we were surrounded by was awful. We could smell cocaine and marihuana being smoked which was the kind of environment we had left behind.

My health began to deteriorate rapidly. This was exacerbated by sleep deprivation because I wasn't able to go to bed at a reasonable hour. Ruby was also struggling but not just as a consequence of the neighbour's behaviour but because of my state of mind – constantly on edge, living on my nerves. Given the effect this was having on her studies, arrangements were made for Ruby to go and live with my mother.

We eventually moved in June 2010 but my health didn't improve. Despite my debilitating illness I managed to get a job working for SWALEC in account management.

My job wasn't the kind where I could take time off whenever I needed. This was because I had somehow become the main source of assistance for vulnerable customers who all seemed to come through to my phone-line. It was strange because there was no particular reason why this should happen.

My colleagues would often get very confused as to why I was receiving all these phone calls. I told them it was God sending these people to me. I knew it was the Lord because He was sending me words of knowledge when I spoke to these customers. My managers were quite happy with the situation and just let me get on with things. It was an amazing time but in the meantime my health was deteriorating by the day.

I received an award from my employers for my excellence in dealing with vulnerable people. I felt as if I was in training to help others outside of my day job in the future.

I took a week off work because I felt so ill and during that time my friends from the City Temple, Adam and Pastor Steve (Ball), took me to hospital. I was diagnosed with deep skeletal pain. When I returned to work the pain just became ten times worse.

At the same time I was in the process of an application to become guardian of a little girl whose mother was going to spend some time at the Teen Challenge Christian Rehabilitation Centre. This is an initiative which focusses on ministering to young people trapped by alcohol and drug addiction.

My application was successful so I planned to resign my job in order to pursue this role. However, before I became involved, the family of the little girl's mother decided to take her into their home. This was great news for the little girl and because I wasn't needed, I remained in my job.

In order to get to work each day I would have to be at the bus stop at 6.15am just to arrive in the office for 8.15am. This forced me to leave Ruby at home and meant that she had to make her own way to school.

I recall standing on the bus stop one morning and speaking to the Lord. I said, 'I am exhausted, this cannot go on, something has got to give and it can't be me.' It was winter time and that week I contracted a flu virus.

As my health deteriorated I became worried about having to give up work and if that happened how I would pay the bills. Who would look after us? I was a single mother.

One night I lay on my bed and prayed, 'Lord, you have to help me.' I heard Him respond by saying, 'Just trust me.'

I'd recently read a testimony about a couple who had given up their livelihood and all their possessions to follow the Lord. The husband was a musician, French by nationality. His wife, who was a French speaker, was a teacher by profession. Whilst out walking, the Frenchman's wife asked her husband if he believed that the Lord would provide for them. Her husband suggested that they should sit on a bench and pray. Then, almost as if it was on cue, two ravens came out of a nearby bush and flew around them, circling their heads. The two birds began making a *'cua'* sound as they flew. Apparently the *'cua'* sound the birds made was distinctly similar to the French word *'croire'* which means believe. It was as if the ravens were saying, 'just believe...believe...believe.'

The following day I was in bed praying to the Lord again for help and He repeated what He'd said the previous night, 'Just trust me.' I was being attacked mentally and needed assurance so I begged Him repeatedly for a sign.

When I'd finished praying I decided to get out of bed and just as I was about to do so, I heard something that caught my attention. I heard two crows outside the window making a *'cua'* sound. I said, 'No way, Lord, no way,' in the sense that I couldn't I believe His sense of humour.

Then the Holy Spirit said to me, 'If you don't resign from your job I'm going to get you sacked!' This will be a controversial statement for some people who will say 'God only blesses and blesses,' but what God was saying was, 'I know what's best for you, girl.'

The next day my manager phoned to see how I was and I procrastinated. I didn't offer to resign. However, the day after that I surrendered, I was too sick to go back to work. I said, 'God, I know that you will look after me no matter what.'

I decided to phone my manager. 'Rebecca,' I said, 'I'm going to have to hand my notice in. I'm sure there are people far more capable of carrying out this job.' I was on a full wage so told her that I felt guilty because someone else could be benefitting from doing my job.

'Thank goodness for that,' said Rebecca. 'A letter was going to be sent to you tomorrow, they are going to terminate your contract.'

I was already signed off sick but this action enabled me to go straight to a benefit agency to tell them how sick I was and ask for help. Leaving my job turned out to be a blessing in disguise because I didn't realise how ill I was.

I was hospitalised again. The symptoms were chest pains, an inability to breathe and being unable to walk properly. I also had a muzzy feeling of confusion in my brain.

Ridiculous notions began to pop into in my head such as, 'I'm dying and I'm on my way out.'

I made an appointment to see my doctor who told me that I had ticked all the boxes of a person suffering with Myalgic Encephalomyelitis (M.E.). He officially diagnosed me as suffering with M.E. on June 20, 2011.

Following her diagnosis, Leonie became housebound, she was trapped by her condition. God in his mercy, however, had sent someone to help her. Ten days prior to Leonie's diagnosis Tim, who had been a close friend for two years, told her that he had feelings for her. Tim became her lifeline. She promptly gave him a key to her home so that he could help to support her. Tim would phone Leonie every day. Sometimes he would just sit on the end of her bed and talk to her. On other occasions he would take her out for a drive in his car or sometimes they would collect her daughter from school.

In July 2011, Tim and I visited the Christian retreat Ffald-y-Brenin. I felt so at peace, the presence of God was clearly there. We spent a few hours there then decided to travel home.

During the journey, Tim asked me something that took the lid off a lot of emotions. That question uncovered a massive pain of rejection from my past and it triggered a lot of pain and hurt. I started to cry for what seemed to be an age. I felt that I was being released. Clearly God was healing me as the layers of the pain of my rejection were being peeled back and exposed.

I remember one particular day being exceptionally bad. I was unable to move, lying face down on my bed in excruciating pain. Tim came over and compassionately laid his hands on me and prayed. I felt a little better and managed to get up and make something to eat. Sometimes prayer would ease the pain and illness but not always.

In August 2011 we decided to get married, as you do in the middle of a tremendous illness. God and I have got a deal, Tim stays in love with me till death us do part and vice versa.

God was very clear about our marriage and gave us many signs indicating that we would eventually be married.

You see we had kissed so that was it...we had to get married! I hadn't planned to kiss Tim or hold his hand until God told me to. It was simple, we've kissed...we need to get married...now!

Leonie was still very sick and throughout September experienced an increase in body pain and aching. She would often be so fatigued that she would fall asleep at the most inopportune times. It happened whilst she was attempting to plan the engagement party and wedding, to which over two hundred guests were invited! I asked how she managed to cope.

The Lord gave me supernatural strength to get through it all, because the wedding was ordained by Him.

After our engagement in October we tried to revisit Ffald-y-Brenin as we felt almost compelled to do so. However, there always seemed to be an obstacle. On one occasion we travelled part of the way there but because of heavy flooding in that area we had to turn back.

We eventually got married in January 2012. What a day, it was amazing! When we were taking our wedding vows I was laughing my head off. We were saying, 'Lord, we've done it all – in sickness and in health, for richer, for poorer, we are poorer – we're skint!'

We were so blessed but on honeymoon I suffered. Virtually every night I was in pain all over my body and would be woken by the intensity of the sensations. One night I had a really severe attack of muscular paralysis. My left arm ceased to function and I experienced horrendous chest pain. I decided to wake Tim because I needed to go to the hospital.

Whenever we stayed away from home we would locate the nearest hospital as a precautionary measure. However, even if I went to hospital the medical staff could do very little to help either through ignorance of the condition or simply because there was no treatment available that had any lasting effect.

Regardless of what I was going through every night I always felt the presence of the Holy Spirit. I would ask over and over again, 'Why am I not being healed? I want to be healed, I want to be healed.'

I would go over these ludicrous ideas in my head that it was my burden, my cross to bear and that sometimes God puts this on you so that you can learn from it. You know…those crazy mixed up doctrines. I didn't believe it for one minute but it would just be in my head. Through it all I knew the Lord would heal me, I just knew it! He saved me from death, this alcoholic crack cocaine addict. I know Him and He knows me, I was convinced He was the only way out.

Although the first week of our honeymoon was horrendous, we were married, we were together. The second week, however, was great. The Lord showed us His provision and taught us about His Kingdom. We saw several miracles happen. He's just amazing!

We returned home from our honeymoon and I guess I just did business with this sickness. I said, 'This has got to go, you have got to go!'

I received many words of knowledge from female friends in Christ who said that God would heal me. I felt assured by their words because I recognised that they were credible sources and I knew that they loved Jesus with all their hearts and minds and I began to stand on His word.

I recall saying to Tim, 'This (illness) just doesn't make sense. The scripture says that *those who wait on the LORD shall renew their strength; they shall mount up with wings like eagles, they shall run and not be weary, they shall walk and not faint,* (Isaiah 40:31).'

I said to the Lord, 'This is not supposed to happen. This is not what I was born to do. It's in my DNA to be well. I wait upon you all the time...how come I'm not well?

One day whilst we were on the way home in the car, I really alarmed Tim when I told him that my legs had stopped working. I said that my chest felt as if it was caving in and that I couldn't breathe. I was in a bad way. I couldn't touch a part of my body that didn't feel like a bruise. I was exhausted. I didn't want to go to the hospital because of the apathy and insensitivity I was invariably met with. I knew they wouldn't understand.

In the past I had been asked, 'Why are you here?' I had often been told to 'go home and take some pain killers.'

Tim overruled me though and took me to the Accident and Emergency department of the Heath Hospital. Tim explained my symptoms to the nurse because I couldn't string a sentence together. She listened and appeared to be sympathetic then dropped the bombshell! She said, 'Apart from that, how do you feel in yourself?'

I was told to go back to my GP who prescribed *Tramadol*, which are strong painkillers. They proved to be largely ineffective because of my high tolerance to medication caused by my previous opiate addiction. However, I became addicted to the *Tramadol* because of fear. I felt unable to cope without medication which was having a psychologically palliative effect upon me.

This was a cunning ploy of the enemy who was deceiving me into believing that I needed a drug which was practically useless in terms of easing my pain. I told my GP that I suspected that I had developed fibromyalgia. I felt that this was probably the reason I was constantly in pain. I was advised to get a second opinion.

Things were pretty desperate. Tim's father was fasting and praying for me. I also knew that Ken and Christalla were doing likewise. I was really careful, however, to keep myself away from some lovely, well-meaning Christians. Why? Let's put it this way. If somebody else had put their hands on me and tried to cast out another demon, I think I would have punched their lights out!

Helen Ball (Pastor Steve Ball's wife) was wonderful. She prayed for me faithfully and was the first one to speak a lot of truth that I was able to receive. She came and prayed with me and said, 'You are a wonderful woman of God. What is happening to you is an attack of the enemy. Steve and I can see that you are running rings around him and he's just desperate to hold you back; so we bind it in Jesus' name.' She was amazing. After that prayer I had a degree of release from the symptoms of my condition.

March arrived and we were desperate to get back to Ffald-y-Brenin. Tim and I had been staying in his father's caravan in West Wales which wasn't too far from there, so we decided to make another visit.

At that time I made a conscious decision not to take any more prescriptions to the chemist for *Tramadol* but still had a few tablets left. So, as we pulled out of the drive to head off to Ffald-y-Brenin, I said, 'Tim, throw them in the bin.'

I felt affirmed to do that. Doing that reminded me of the time five years previously when I had been diagnosed with the bi-polar condition. I'd thrown the tablets away in faith but went backwards and forwards to the bin just looking at them thinking, 'Have I done the right thing?' But God said, 'Just trust me.' So I assured myself that He'd done it before so He will do it again.

A week prior to making this trip to Ffald-y-Brenin we went to stay at Tim's parents' house.

We went on a shopping trip to Abergavenny but I couldn't walk very far because the soles of my feet hurt so much. I couldn't breathe, my body was aching and it was awful.

When we got back to the house Tim's father was cleaning his car. The others went into the house but I stayed outside and helped Tim's father a little. Generally, if I was having a good day I would try and do a few things but this hadn't been a good day and I hadn't taken heed.

When Tim and I got home I was absolutely shattered! I managed to get upstairs and got into bed fully clothed. I sat there and my heart started to cramp. I had been getting similar symptoms and palpitations since December.

I called Ruby and Tim to the bedroom. 'Come and sit on the bed,' I said, 'I need to talk to you. Now before you scream and shout and tell me that I'm being stupid, I want you to know that if anything happens to me, I want you both to stay in touch. Ruby, I want you to allow Tim's parents to be grandparents to you, they love you so much and Tim and Ruby you have to promise to always love each other.'

I basically prepared them for the worst. I honestly didn't think I was going to make the year out but to see me in church on a Sunday, standing, worshiping and praising, no one would have any inkling that I was sick. I would try my best to get through the session but when my body was failing I would ask the Lord to strengthen me and He always did.

Of course they both tried to dismiss what I was saying. Ruby said, 'Don't be stupid, mum, I don't want to talk about this, it's not going to happen.' I looked them both in the eye. 'I don't think this thing is going to leave me until it takes me,' I said.

I spoke to the Lord and said, 'If there is a purpose for me, heal me and keep me alive, if not take me, I'm ready now. Either heal me for the purposes you have for me or take me home – it's okay.'

Finally we made it! We got to Ffald-y-Brenin. We journeyed there via the GPS systems on our mobile phones and also by directions from the local people because we didn't have a satellite navigation system. We'd owned one previously but we had to get rid of it. We would have got divorced before the wedding if we hadn't!

An amazing thing happened on the way to Ffald-y-Brenin. We stopped at a petrol station and asked for directions because we were approaching from a different direction to the way we had previously driven. During the journey we passed through an area that really looked familiar to me but I couldn't for the life of me remember the place I was thinking of. However, a little further on, I knew the way – I just knew and got us there.

As we were approaching the retreat we could both tell the lightness in the air, it made us feel so close to God.

After parking we went into the bookstore. There was a man there called Ivan, who was about to conduct a tour of the retreat for a group of people.

He was lovely. He reminded me of my Dad. I remember thinking this is what my Dad would be like if he was saved. He asked us if we'd been shown around previously. We hadn't, so upon his invitation we joined the tour.

There was a lady in the tour group who asked us what our names were and where we were from. As we talked there was something about her, we just couldn't take our eyes off her. When we asked where she was from she said, 'Yorkshire,' but she said this in a really strong Carmarthen accent. Tim said, 'Not with an accent like that you're not.'

She told us that her name was Sue and that she was originally from a place called Ammanford, which is near Swansea. Then it came to me! This was the place I couldn't remember the name of. The name should have rolled off my tongue because after completing my degree, I'd lived in Swansea for seven years.

This lady had that prophet stare… the kind of stare that goes right through you, into your bones, that makes you want to say, please don't look at me anymore. However, she was a lovely…lovely lady.

After the guided tour Tim and I parted for a while to allow me some time alone. I had just about had enough and wanted to let go of everything. I wanted to go and worship God and read, I like to do that, so I went and sat in the book shop and Tim went into the prayer room where there was a piano.

I think it was Roy Godwin's wife, Daphne, who came in to replenish the stock in the book shop. Do you know what? I couldn't even speak to her. I think I said, 'Hi, it's really busy here', and that was it. I'll talk to anyone, so this was a very strange thing for me to do.

I saw Tim looking for me but I dodged him. I had just stepped out of the toilet but I backed in again. I didn't want to see him.

I said to God, 'I don't want to talk to anyone...I don't want to look at anyone...I don't want to do anything. I'm not going to move from this spot unless you heal me or take me. If I die here, that's fine.'

Tim finally found me. He snuck up on me! He said, 'Ah, there you are – come on, let's get a cup of tea.' I didn't want to move but eventually relented. We went into the craft room and sat looking out of the gallery window across the beautiful Gwaun valley.

Sue was in there with her husband, her children and two friends. We chatted for a while then the adults went into the prayer room next door, leaving the children to play with us. We found that we couldn't stop talking to their little boy who was amazing. He was such a godly child. He had such a clean countenance. We were fascinated by his meticulous brush strokes as he painted his little figurines.

As I was drinking a cup of tea I felt as if a huge, heavy wet blanket had lifted off me but somehow it was still hovering just behind me.

I remember thinking, 'Lord, what was that?' Then I felt as if a huge claw ripped it away from me.

During the week leading up to the visit to Ffald-y-Brenin Leonie told me that she'd experienced some strange sensations in addition to heart spasms and palpitations. Leonie said that she felt as if a spike was embedded in her scalp on the left side of her body. 'The best way to describe it' she explained, 'was as if a splinter was lodged in my head, side and leg.'

We were really at home with those children but as soon as the adults re-entered the room I motioned to Tim to pull his chair around to face me. 'I can't have another conversation with adults who don't know what they're talking about,' I thought. I was done with small talk, with making new friends. As far as I was concerned I was 'checking out.' I simply couldn't be bothered.

As Tim and I sat facing each other I was drawn to a little *aloe vera* plant and began to play with its leaves. Just at that moment the Holy Spirit said to me, 'That lady is going to minister to you, you are going to be released.'

I sort of shrugged my shoulders and said in a rather nonchalant manner, 'Really! You know what…it's over to you, Lord. I'm done standing…I'm done fighting. I can't do this anymore. If she's got a word from you, Lord, I really hope it's from you. If she's going to lay hands on me, it had better be kosher.'

Sue and her husband caught our attention because they started to talk about Teen Challenge. As I mentioned earlier in my story, I was going to look after a little girl to allow her mother to participate in Teen Challenge, hence that organisation is very close to my heart. Sue's conversation with her husband and the others drifted towards Swansea and the aptly named Wine Street, which is a boozer's hotspot. They lauded the street pastors for the amazing work they were doing for God there.

Having been a former boozer I also used to go to Wine Street. My familiarity with Swansea was partly the reason Tim and I got drawn into the discussion. We began to share details about our respective occupations, what God had called us to do and talked about our work as worship leaders in the City Temple.

It transpired that Sue had some friends in Yorkshire who were also worship leaders. They were looking for an open air venue for a concert, so we had a commonality between us. It was almost as if we'd known each other for years.

We started to talk about the ministry God had called us into and the pastoral care work we would like to get involved in but then I mentioned that I couldn't do so because I'd been so sick.

I tried to avoid elaborating about my illness but Sue was like a dog with a bone; she wouldn't let it go.

'If you don't mind me asking,' she said, 'what are you sick with?'

Tim looked at me knowingly. He knew I didn't want to discuss my illness with yet another person. I reluctantly responded whilst carefully avoiding any eye contact.

'I have been diagnosed with M.E. and Fibromyalgia,' I said with a huge sigh.

'I knew it!' she said. 'The Lord healed me of that. I know exactly where you are. I was looking at you, I could see you were wasting away. I can see it was all over you. But no more! Can I pray for you?'

I told her that the Holy Spirit had already told me that she was going to minister to me.

'He told me too,' said Tim.

'Me too!' she said. 'So that's it then.'

'Okay, Sue, you can pray for me,' I said with an air of resignation. I tell you, she shot out of that chair. The way she ministered to me was just phenomenal.

Sue began by holding my hand and affirming my identity in God. Then she was on her knees before me and looked into my face and commanded an orphan spirit to leave me.

'Get lost, get away from her!' she said. 'She is a child of the Most High God.' This was a pivotal moment because I remember telling Tim during the previous day how loved I'd felt by his parents. Sadly though, I had not felt loved by my own parents, well not both at the same time. Through not wanting to dishonour my parents, I won't divulge any more. They did the best that they could with what they had at the time. I love them dearly, they are fantastic people.

My mother is a born again Christian and my dad's getting there. My parents were very young when they had me so it was very relevant when Sue had stood against the 'orphan spirit' in me and sent it back to where it came from.

Sue's female friend was stood behind me and touched me gently on the shoulder.

'Can I ask you a personal question?' she said. 'Do you feel fought for or protected by your father or any other male figure in your life?' 'No...no I don't,' I replied.

I told her that although I have a great dad and he did the best he could, there were times he could have done better. I told her how I had become involved in relationship after relationship where men were just horrendous towards me. I'd had to fight the whole time from my childhood upwards. I even fought fisticuff fights. I never fought a woman, only men. So no, I never felt protected, I always felt let down by men in my life.

The woman began to pray for Leonie and a gut wrenching sob emerged from deep within her. As she wept, the Holy Spirit instructed Leonie to stretch her legs out. Then the most amazing thing happened...

I felt the affliction pushing downwards and out through my feet. The woman who had just prayed for me could see what was happening.

'This thing is going to go out through your legs,' she remarked. I told her that the Holy Spirit had just spoken to me and said the same thing. He'd given me a word telling me exactly what was going to happen!

I received further prayer and ministry and God honoured Tim for standing by me in sickness and in health. The word was, 'you are a man who can be trusted.' Tim had previously received that word of knowledge and several times since.

Leonie Riley

During the process of being ministered to I began to think that Sue and the others were angels. When their prayers ended, Sue, her husband, the children and their friends all walked down the Ffald-y-Brenin drive towards the Cwm Gwaun valley and seemed to disappear. They were gone! However, it later became apparent that they were human after all, because a short while later Sue and I emailed each other.

After leaving the craft room we felt the Lord say, 'Walk to the cross and lay down.'

We walked along the bridal path as far as the bench and I knew that the appropriate thing to do was to take my shoes and socks off. I walked to the cross and touched the bottom of it and said, 'Jesus, I give it all, take everything, take all I have, it's yours.'

I looked down into the briar bushes – well I think they were briar. 'They are strange looking bushes, they're so spiky,' I thought to myself. 'Why do they exist around the cross? Why don't they have lush green leaves?'

Tim snapped me out of my thought processes by beginning to read from Hebrews 5. The teaching illustrates how much of an honour it is to come before the throne of God and worship Him because of His sacrifice of His Son. So that's what we did. We stood there thanking and loving Him, we were just laying everything down.

We decided to go and sit on the bench and gazed at the cross. At that moment I heard a sound coming from the bushes. I asked Tim if he'd heard anything and he said he hadn't. 'I thought okay that was a sign just for me.'

Then I heard what I know was the voice of the Holy Spirit. The voice sounded like the wind. He came through the bushes towards me. He encircled me and the sounds in this wind were so off the scale in pitch it was incredible. It sounded like the ring of a bell but there were also, what I can only describe as many bells. Then I heard just one word, 'love.' Deep within my spirit I heard the words, 'I love you, I will never leave you, I will never forsake you, you're mine, I'm yours, you're my beloved, you are assured, you are in the right place at the right time, you are carrying the mantle I have given you correctly, I'm coming back for you, you can release everything you need to release to me, I'm never going to leave your side.'

The Holy Spirit continued to encircle me. That was for me to hear, no one else. I felt beautiful...and released...and assured. Just totally in love with Jesus.

When it was time to leave we didn't want to go. We eventually got into the car and sat there totally amazed – we were speechless.

We'd bought the audio version of the book *The Grace Outpouring* by Roy Godwin, and listened to it on the way back to the caravan.

I didn't recall a thing about the journey home, but in the morning I could make a fist with both hands. It was amazing! I hadn't been able to do that for so long. I could put my feet flat on the floor without pain and go to the toilet without any problems. Things most people take for granted.

We went to Tim's parents' house to tell them the good news and we were so excited. I remember bouncing up and down saying, 'I've received my healing, He's healed me, He's healed me!'

The enormity of the healing took a while to be fully realised in Tim and myself because it was almost as if we were both appearing in the same dream.

We stayed overnight at Tim's parents' house and when we woke Tim said, 'Love, your back, it's completely flat! There's nothing there!'

Prior to my healing my body would warn me if I was due a terrible day (which was most days at that time). The base of my spine would be very soft and would flare up, almost like a cushion. So much so that Tim would always notice the swelling. We went down to breakfast and I announced to Tim's parent's that I was well and felt amazing.

During the next few days the enemy would come and flirt. He said, 'Come on, Leonie, did God really heal you? Were you really ever sick?'

I didn't get into any debate. I would just respond with God's word. I said, 'It is written, *I am the Lord, I am your healer and those that wait upon the Lord shall not grow weary, they shall walk and not faint, they will rise up...* I will rise up on wings of an eagle. Get lost. This healing is mine! By His stripes I am healed. He didn't take the stripes for nothing, I'm healed and I'm taking it now!'

Leonie quoted Matthew 11:12, 'The Kingdom of Heaven suffers violence and the violent it takes by storm.' She explained that the English-Greek translation of this is 'Apadso.' This describes those who tenaciously dig their heels in, those who press in and wrench the power from Heaven. Leonie certainly did this! She invaded the enemy's kingdom with her Father's kingdom.

This victorious speech sounds easy but I can assure you that it's not. You have got to stand in the power of God, you have to walk in it. Christalla gave me a copy of a prayer to claim my healing.

She said, 'You have to use this whenever the enemy deceives you into thinking the symptoms have re-appeared.' I have a confession to make, I read it once. However, the truth of that prayer grasped me on the inside. When I read it I said, 'Yes, yes...this is mine! Enemy you can get lost. Jesus died for me and by His stripes I'm healed.' All those assertions were constantly flowing from me.

Where is Your Faith? – Just Believe!

Since the healing I've had a few off days but only one really bad one. On that particular day I felt so ill I could hardly get out of bed. I eventually did manage it though and verbalised the words, 'This is mine, this is my healing, you didn't die for nothing Lord.' It took me a while to get through that day but I did it.

It's a really strange thing having to walk in your healing. People have said to me, 'You mustn't say that you are struggling, you mustn't say that you are still sick.'

I would reply, 'Well what should I say?' I was told to say that I am victorious in Christ.

Well, I live the victory! I'm standing here in His victory, although I sometimes don't feel victorious. I used to stand in His victory up on the podium every Sunday morning singing my heart out whilst I was fatigued and in constant pain. I refused to give in. Whether His will was to heal me or take me home, the victory would still be His. He would still be victorious. This is why He died and was resurrected so that I could live out His promises on earth and show the world who He is.

I tell you, I burn with passion for Jesus, I always have but what I feel for the Lord has intensified since the healing.

The first thing the Lord healed was my mind of the 'dodgy doctrines' sourced from the lies of the enemy who says, 'this is your burden to carry…this is yours to bear…God puts this stuff on you to teach you something.'

Really! God is good and gives us the Holy Spirit without measure. If those who are evil wouldn't give a scorpion to their children if they asked for bread, how much more then is your Father going to give to you who is good? It is not in His nature to hurt us. I was not about to accept those lies, it was the first thing that had to go – 'stinking' thinking. That doctrine was healed in me.

Whenever I become aware of an individual struggling with sickness who tells me that he or she believes that their illness is God's way of teaching them a lesson or that He's keeping them sick to make them dependent upon Him, I can't fix that. If the person believes that particular doctrine, I leave it to that person to seek God with all their mind, soul, spirit and whatever they have left in strength.

I would only intervene to address that doctrine if I was led by the Holy Spirit to do so. The sensitivity with which we have to approach people who are struggling with illnesses is tremendous. No one has a true understanding unless they themselves have been in a similar situation.

I would strongly suggest that those who have no understanding of a debilitating illness leave ministry to those who have inside knowledge, those who have 'been there.'

Christalla didn't say to me, 'address this or address that.' I wasn't asked to go through a step by step process, she just held me and I cried. Christalla didn't try to provide answers she just prayed with me. She simply put a loving arm around me and said, 'I know.'

Sue, the lady who ministered to me before the Holy Spirit healed me, said, 'I know…I know where you are at.'

Sue told me about her times of desperation when she was ill, times when she had been at home sat on her stairs or at the kitchen table, unable to move, unable to function, unable to even feed her children.

Given that she understood, I had allowed her to minister to me. We need to have an awareness we can't just go wading in. We need to educate people. We need to let those who are suffering with M.E./Fibromyalgia know that there is somewhere to go, a place where they will be understood; a place where the sufferer won't be judged or condemned, a place where their fragility and mental state will be acknowledged, and taken into account.

I want to finish my testimony by saying I just want give The Lord the glory for everything He has done for me. Praise His Holy Name!

'The Lord is near to all who call on him, to all who call on him in truth. He fulfils the desire of those who fear him he also hears their cry and saves them,' Psalm 145:18-19.

It was Friday, April 13, the day before my marriage to Christalla. We arrived at the City Temple church for our wedding practice in the early afternoon. As we approached the main auditorium entrance we heard singing. We recognised the voice as belonging to Leonie but she sounded different. As we walked through the door we were amazed by how beautiful the wedding decorations were. Leonie had graciously blessed us by offering to decorate the church for us as a wedding present. She also sang at our wedding so we were doubly blessed. I looked around and asked who had helped her because a lot of work had been done. She jumped up and down as she joyfully told us that she had done it all entirely on her own because she was now able to. She had been healed two days previously at Ffald-y-Brenin! What a testimony this was of God's love, compassion and healing power. Two women who had both suffered terribly for years with the same illness had been set free. Thank you Lord, bless Your Holy name.

6

Aled Power

Aled has a compassion for the disadvantaged and is committed
to working with homeless people. He often works in collaboration
with other volunteers but for many years has singlehandedly
ministered to people who are sleeping rough on the streets.

This is Aled's story:

I spent the first eighteen years of my life in Newport. Every
Sunday we attended church as a family. As I look back I'm
thankful that I was grounded in the Bible from a young age. At
the time, however, I spent most of those church services wishing I
was elsewhere. The streets outside the church seemed far more
interesting than the aisles inside. I was baptised at the age of
thirteen but gradually drifted away from the church.

By the time I moved to university I was far more likely to be in
the pub than the church, reading anarchist magazines or eastern
philosophy rather than the Bible, and singing Johnny Rotten
rather than John Newton. Not surprisingly, my life soon became a
little messy.

At my brother's suggestion I reluctantly found myself back in
church. Over the following months, with the help of some key
individuals, I discovered a God whose arms are always wide open

to His stumbling prodigals (Luke 15:20) and who loves us as we are and not as we should be.

As I grew in my awareness of God's love for me it seemed a natural response to want to extend that love towards others. So with a Christian friend I began visiting those 'sleeping rough' on the streets of Cardiff.

Since then I've seen numerous examples of God's grace and protection…

One night, as we were visiting the guys on the street, we came to a lane we visited every week. For no reason we could explain we decided this week not to venture down the lane. It transpired that everyone who had ventured down the lane that night had been assaulted with a baseball bat…

Another time I returned from work to discover our house had been burgled. The burglar had been around the bedrooms taking anything valuable in sight, including, laptops, i-Pods and other electrical equipment. My room was the only one with no way of locking it, yet strangely, I was the only person who had nothing taken!

I love that verse by the poet James Russell Lowell:

Truth forever on the scaffold, Wrong forever on the throne –
Yet that scaffold sways the future, and, behind the dim unknown,
Standeth God within the shadow, keeping watch above His own.

Whenever we show compassion and care for others God blesses us in so many ways. Aled has for many years and unbeknown to anyone else, ventured out onto the streets in all weathers to feed and help the poor. In the first instance, I believe that Aled has been protected because our Lord is true to His word. 'The thief does not come except to steal, and to kill and to destroy. I have come that they may have life, and that they may have it more abundantly,' (John 10:10). And secondly, he was blessed because

Aled Power

Jesus says, 'I was hungry and you gave me something to eat, I was thirsty and you gave me something to drink, I was a stranger and you invited me in, I needed clothes and you clothed me, I was sick and you looked after me, I was in in prison and you visited me...Truly I tell you, whatever you did for one of the least of these brothers and sisters of mine, you did for me,' (Matthew 25:35-36;40). Amen.

Where is Your Faith? – Just Believe!

7

Adey Adegbite

Adey is a God fearing woman with a wonderful heart to serve the Lord. She was born in London to Nigerian parents who migrated to this country in the 1960s. Her parents brought her up in the Anglican Church which she attended for many years. Adey is now a born again Christian who attends the City Temple Church. She is a Team leader of the Foodbank team which operates from the City Temple. Adey has another volunteer role as a committee member of Cardiff Consortium of Charities, who recycle and supply used furniture and appliances to disadvantaged people. Adey was a previous member of the Homeless Outreach Team.

Here's Adey's story:

In the 1980s Pentecostal Christians were widely referred to as 'happy clappies.' At that time my parents were very anti-Pentecostal. Many Christians of other denominations were dubious about Pentecostal beliefs with regards to the empowerment of the spiritual gifts such as speaking in tongues and divine healing. At that time a few high profile newspaper stories emerged which portrayed a very negative image of the Pentecostal movement.

I recall listening to a sermon in my church whereby the minister was talking about how he believed that he had received the Holy

Ghost. This was the first time I'd heard an Anglican minister talk about the Holy Spirit. I remember thinking, 'I want to experience that too.' There was a quickening within me, a hunger for the Holy Spirit. I began to consider whether or not to leave the Anglican Church to become a Pentecostal and asked the Lord for direction. I said, 'Lord, how do I know that they (Pentecostals) are not just a bunch of nutcases? I need to be sure.'

The Lord didn't keep me waiting too long before answering my question and did so in an amazing way. I was having the worst menstrual pain I had ever experienced in my life. The landlady of the house I was living in at the time had to go out shopping but was reluctant to leave me because I was in agony. I went down on my knees and said, 'Lord, if this Pentecostal church is of you then show me.'

In an instant, heat shot through my body from the top of my head to my feet followed by coldness. The pain disappeared immediately. I got to my feet and started jumping up and down. I was healed! I touched the floor thinking it would be wet because of the energy that went through my body, but it was dry. This was an answer to prayer. How could anyone who had an experience like this doubt that it was from God. I had my answer. The Pentecostal Church was the way for me.

I found a Pentecostal church in Aldgate, London, but lived quite a distance from there in Hackney. In order to get to that church I had to use an underground train and also a bus.

My parents had told me to be home that first night by 11pm, but I was late leaving the church. It was now 10.55pm! I had five minutes to get home and a forty five minute journey ahead of me. As I waited for the bus which would take me direct to Hackney I prayed, 'Lord, you did it for Hezekiah, you can do it for me, you can stop time.'

I boarded the bus and was the only passenger. There was no traffic in front of us, no one at the bus stops, all the traffic lights stayed green without me praying for that to happen. I simply quoted God's word and kept saying, 'Lord, you did it for Hezekiah, you have to stop time for me.'

When we arrived I got off the bus and ran and ran and as I got through the door my mom said, 'Oh, you're on time. Your nose...it's red...you're glowing.' I was electrified, I was buzzing. God had actually stopped time for me! A forty five minute journey had taken just five! (2 Kings 20:9-11).

Here is another amazing miracle. I went into a phone booth to ring my parents. I'd used all the money I had in my purse for the phone call and put the empty purse on top of the coin box. During the conversation with my parents, I happened to mention that I was completely broke. When I finished the call I took my purse and was about to close it when I noticed something that totally amazed me. My purse contained a five pound note!

Adey lodged in Cardiff to study Laboratory Science. One day, she and two student friends decided to visit Castell Coch, which is one of Cardiff's major tourist attractions. Whilst they were there they met some young Christian men. During conversation they discovered that the young men were members of the United Pentecostal Church (UPC), which was in the Llanrumney area of Cardiff. Adey and her friend Mary, accepted an invitation to attend the UPC. As Adey was Anglican and Mary was from a Catholic background they found Pentecostal worship quite dissimilar to what they had been used to. However, Adey and Mary enjoyed the service so much that they decided to attend regularly.

I recall fasting and praying for ten days, asking God to help me make a decision about whether or not to leave home and settle in Cardiff. I did this because of the opposition I got from my parents when I disclosed to them that I was contemplating leaving the Anglican Church. In Nigerian culture the children stay at home at home until they marry.

One day God told me to up and leave, so that was it for me. I packed a suitcase, left a note and left. I ran away from home. Although God was clearly instrumental in the whole process, that was the most difficult decision I have ever made in my life.

I believe that it was no accident that I ended up studying in Wales...that my friends and I chose to go to Castell Coch for the day...that we met a Pentecostal pastor's son and his friends who witnessed to three strangers, two of whom decide to attend and eventually join their church. A church I attended for around ten years until it closed.

As time went by I slowly began to build bridges with my parents. This proved to be an extremely difficult process but I praise God because my mother has become a Pentecostal, as have my sister and most of my cousins.

Adey related two stories of divine healings she received in August 2012.

One Saturday night I was in the City Temple assisting the Homeless Outreach Project. I was in the kitchen washing up when a guy asked me if I wanted a cup of coffee with milk. I don't recall his name. I declined and explained why I couldn't accept his offer. I told him that I had been lactose intolerant for about twenty years and was not able to partake of dairy products. He told me that he and some friends recently prayed for a person who'd had the same condition and the individual was healed.

He got really excited because he'd experienced God healing this condition and wanted to see it happen again. He asked me if I wanted him to pray for me. I agreed, but because we were so busy we didn't get around to it immediately.

Later, at the end of the evening, we had our coats on and were about to leave when he suddenly remembered his offer to pray for me. It wasn't a long prayer, only around two minutes. When he finished praying, I thanked him and we went our separate ways.

About a week later I went to a midweek meeting at the City Temple and was offered a cup of coffee with milk. I didn't hesitate and thought, 'I have been claiming my healing, I am healed I can have one,' and did.

As I slowly swallowed the liquid my throat began to scratch. This was an indication that a physical reaction to the milk was imminent. However, I had faith that I had been divinely healed and just repeatedly said to myself, 'in Jesus' name, in Jesus' name,' until the symptoms disappeared.

Prior to my healing the consumption of milk would cause the following sequence; bumps all over my body, a scratching in my throat, a feeling of nausea, a swollen stomach, my stomach would then make noises not too dissimilar to a coffee percolator, then diarrhoea would follow. I have had no recurrence of the condition. Thank you Lord!

The previous week I had attended a church meeting in the Cathays area of Cardiff where the teaching focussed on us not trying to put restrictions on God and how we shouldn't try to compartmentalise him. That's why I agreed to the offer of prayer for the lactose intolerance. In the past I had used this condition as a means of restricting and controlling my diet; it gave me an excuse not to eat. It was all part of a control process. I would refuse food on the basis that I might react to it. These were just excuses. I needed to simply hand it all over to God.

Adey had also been suffering with a painful foot condition for four years. She told me that the ligaments in the arches of her feet had crystallised and been causing excruciating pain in her feet, calves, legs and thighs.

Prior to becoming affected with this condition Adey had been a keen walker but had been forced to give this up because of the constant pain. In July 2012 Adey was signed off sick from work for twelve weeks due to being unable to cope with the pain in her feet.

It was in early August that I told Adey about an event Christalla and I were planning at the Llanishen Community Shop/City Temple Church (North). We were going to invite a Pastor Brian Cresswell and his wife Mary to speak and also conduct a healing ministry session. I told her that Brian and Mary had been serving the Lord with their healing and deliverance ministry for over twenty years. They had travelled extensively working in far flung places such as Africa, India, Brazil and the Philippines. I invited Adey her to come along and she agreed.

I attended the meetings with the intention of seeking prayer to help me to forgive myself for some personal issues. When I went forward for ministry, that is what I asked for, but I also mentioned that I had some on-going health problems without declaring what they were. Pastor Brian said that it was important for me to be able to forgive myself and prayed for that but also prayed for my health issues. I really can't remember if I was specific about the problems with my feet but he said that I would be healed within three weeks.

During those three weeks I thanked God every day for my healing and simply claimed it. Every time I felt a twinge of pain I would just reject it in Jesus' name. Then, as Pastor Brian prophesied, I was healed within three weeks.

Gradual healing was a completely different experience for me because in the past I have received prayer for healing and it has occurred immediately. A few years ago, I had a problem with my hip for which I received prayer and the problem was healed immediately, therefore, my expectation was that this would always be the case.

Adey Adegbite

Adey told me about another miracle that took place many years ago, whilst she was baby-sitting two small children for a Pentecostal Christian family. The children's grandfather was the pastor of the church.

I was playing with one of the children, who at the time was a three year old boy (this boy is now grown up and has three children of his own). He accidently banged my head on the floor and I began to slur my words. I realised that I was concussed, given that this had happened to me previously. Then something incredible happened!

The little boy placed his hand on the injured area of my head and said, 'In Jesus' name.' Those were the only words he uttered and I returned to full consciousness.

The little boy had witnessed his grandfather, his parents and others in the church laying hands on each other and simply replicated what he had seen. The funny thing was that he did this because he wanted me to carry on playing with him. At that tender age he somehow understood that prayer was an effective tool and used it. Amazing!

'Even a child is known by his deeds,' (Proverbs 20:11).

Where is Your Faith? – Just Believe!

8

Lloyd Jelinek

I am twenty nine years old and was born and brought up in in a Christian family in Aberdare, South Wales. We worshipped at the Mission Church which was a non-denominational, free-church.

As a child I was always in tune with God, I was always the one who knew all the answers in Sunday school. I was quite blessed because my parents bought me a bible when I was really young and I used to go to the church summer schools. This gave me a good depth of knowledge of the bible.

We moved away from Aberdare when I was eleven and we began to attend the Bethel church at Llantwit Major. It was around that time that I began to resent going to church. I just wanted to be with my mates doing the kind of things they enjoyed. I started to consume alcohol and around that time I got drunk for the first time. I was twelve or thirteen when I tried weed (cannabis). I wanted worldly things, drink, drugs and girls – anything but church which had become so boring for me. I just wanted to go out and sin because that was what my friends were doing. I just wanted to fit in, to be normal, I felt alone.

The weed really gripped me. From the first time I tried it I loved it. I started to sell it in the school. I was the first one in my year to sell weed. I went off the rails, I was a bit crazy. I was the 'nutty' kid would do anything for attention, who loved to make other people laugh. My friends and I would steal chocolate bars and booze from the local shops and we would be drinking at 8am in the morning behind the rugby club before going to school. I remember a local police officer, PC Bennett, picking us up and taking us to school while we were still drunk. We'd break into people's caravans which were empty during the winter, to take drugs. We were up to all sorts of nonsense.

I eventually got expelled from school at fifteen for being drunk and smashing up other people's GCSE art work. Thankfully, my father persuaded the school to allow me back to do my exams.

Being absent from school gave me the excuse to sell even more drugs and I became the biggest drug dealer of pills and weed in Llantwit. I really loved my drugs, namely cannabis, speed and magic mushrooms. By the age of sixteen I was selling loads of bags of 100 ecstasy tablets and half kilos of weed every three days, I was even going into the pubs selling them. I was a mess.

At that time I had £1,000 worth of pills and hash stolen from me. I'd stashed the drugs in my room at home and my mother found them. She left a note saying, 'I don't want an explanation Lloyd, just get them out of the house.'

I had to find a hiding place for the drugs so in my wisdom I took them down the street and placed them in a hole in a wall. Someone followed me and helped themselves. I was so 'off my head' on pills I didn't realise that it wasn't a safe place to hide the drugs. I had an arrangement with my dealer whereby I would get the drugs 'on tick' and pay him when I sold the gear. Fortunately for me my supplier found out who stole the drugs and because that person had also stolen from him, he let me off...thankfully.

I was still sixteen when I got myself a carpentry apprenticeship which I managed to mess up so I went to live with my mates in Cardiff. I didn't come home, I just stayed there for months doing drugs. My parents were really worried and tried to persuade me to return home but I refused. I was just a stupid kid who was so blinded by the drug culture that I just wanted to be 'drugged up' all the time.

I eventually returned to Llantwit but continued taking drugs, I'd have drugs every day. I was a big 'pot head' but would take any drugs going. I had a few jobs but didn't keep them for very long. In between times I would be selling drugs but even when I was working I was smoking so much weed that I would sell the stuff on the side to get free smokes.

My mother had sleeping tablets and I used to steal them, I stole other things from both parents, I even stole from a church once. Things just got darker and darker over the years.

When I was eighteen I met my first girlfriend Becky. I was working in a supermarket in Cowbridge as a supervisor. I went out with her for a few years and that calmed me down a bit. We'd go out drinking to clubs and pubs but that was about it. Becky didn't do drugs so I began to take less of them.

At this point I need to share something really important with you. The trouble is that because I did so many drugs over the years I can't remember absolutely everything that happened. However, during the time when I was sixteen and visiting my mates in Cardiff, I'd been smoking huge amounts of weed one day. I remember that my mouth was really dry and I went into a side room and whilst I was there God said something to me. The exact words I can't remember but it was something like… 'I will lead you' somewhere or other…'to righteousness…and I will make you drink.' Then amazingly bursts of water came into my mouth. It was unreal.

I then went back into the room and started to talk about God all night. It was weird me doing this because I was talking about the Lord whilst still being stoned. My mate got annoyed with me and told me to shut up. That was my first proper encounter with God, but I didn't build on it. I just carried on partying, clubbing, raving, drinking and taking drugs now and then.

I split up with Becky, drifted in and out of jobs and started selling drugs again. However, each time I got a girlfriend I would calm down. I began working away from home and as I got older drugs became less appealing. I had basically done every drug under the sun. I'd tried heroin once, crack cocaine once, loads of powder (cocaine) and loads of pills. I still had the awareness not to get into heroin or crack cocaine because that stuff really messes people's lives up.

Lloyd was now twenty six and still dealing drugs. He would buy his drugs from his supplier in Newport and sell them on. One day, he had just got off the train at Cardiff station having returned from Newport when he had a chance meeting with a girl whom he'd known in the past. Her name was Nikita. Lloyd continued...

In those days I would use her for casual sex and then just dump her. This happened a few times. Anyway, after this chance encounter at the train station we got together and she eventually became my fiancée.

I got into poker and eventually became a semi-professional player whilst at the same time, selling drugs for a living. As I got older, I scaled down from using the heavier drugs but I always smoked weed. I was renowned for it.

We'd been together for a year and a half when we decided to leave the UK for a while. We wanted somewhere cheap and hot. The idea was that I would support us by playing internet poker, so it didn't matter where we went. We researched several countries looking for warm climates and low crime rates. We eventually decided on Goa in India. This place was going to be ideal. It was great for the drug culture and party lifestyle.

Lloyd Jelinek

Nine months prior to Lloyd and Nikita going to Goa they had attended his grandfather's funeral. Lloyd's grandfather had emigrated from Czechoslovakia to the UK and become a born again Christian. Unbeknown to Lloyd at the time was the fact that his grandfather had regularly attended the City Temple in Cardiff. People at the Temple referred to him as 'the bouncing Czech', because of his gregarious, outgoing nature. Lloyd was devastated by his grandfather's death. He felt an enormous amount of guilt because he believed that he hadn't been a big enough feature in his grandfather's life.

When I think back I should have visited my grandfather more often, I should have been more involved in his life, but at that time I was in a spiritually dark place. Nikita and I funded the trip to India and the purchase of my laptop computer with some of the money that was left to me in my grandfather's will. I think he must have blessed that money because moving abroad and researching conspiracy theories/religions on the laptop, led me to the Lord.

So we moved to Goa for six months and settled in fairly quickly. We loved the routine. I was earning plenty of money and things were great.

One day, I had the opportunity of entering a major professional event, *The Poker Stars Goa Tour*. So I entered the preliminary qualifying rounds but began to lose with the most ridiculous bad hands. I ended up punching the computer. I couldn't understand it. Nikita begged me to stop playing. I eventually saw sense and ceased to play.

Given that it was monsoon (the rainy season) there wasn't a lot available to occupy our minds so we began to research things on the internet. We had an interest in looking at the *Illuminati* conspiracy theory which is in my opinion, conspiracy fact. The rationale is that the world is run on a satanic agenda.

We had a friend, Pete, who I used to meet up with in a local bar. Pete shared our interest in conspiracy theories so we had great discussions. One day, we began to discuss Noah's flood and Pete, who wasn't a Christian, told us that it had been scientifically proven that the flood had actually happened.

Now this stuck in my head for some reason, so we began to research different religions. We looked at Hinduism and the Mayan calendar which predicted the end of the world in 2012, but mainly conspiracy theories. We were struck how everything seemed to come back to the Bible and we started looking at the end times prophecy of the book of Revelation.

I can't recall exactly what we were watching on TV but on this particular day something clicked and God gave me the gift of faith. I can't explain it, but I just knew the bible was real. It was God putting me on the right path. Nikita realised too and said, 'What are we going to do?'

When we were about to go to sleep that night I prayed in my heart, 'Lord, I know you are there...I know that I am a sinner...save me.' So I said the sinner's prayer and asked the Lord to forgive me and come into my life. This time He wasn't letting me go and something happened which I will never experience again until I get to glory.

When John the Baptist said, *'after me comes one who is more powerful than I...He will baptise you with the Holy Spirit and fire,'* it was just like that. The fear of God went through me. My bones shook inside me...I can't really describe it. I was overwhelmed and I cried and prayed all night. I changed.

The next morning I got up, got on my moped (everyone hires them over there) and went to find a church. There are only Roman Catholic churches in Goa, there are no born again Christians out there. So I found a church and went inside. I went into a little side room and there were a few people praying. I saw some Bibles on a shelf and picked one up which had a book mark placed at the beginning of Romans 1 and I read the whole of the chapter. I was just crying, overwhelmed in the spirit. God was speaking to me and I just knew I was a sinner.

Whilst I was crying the Indians were looking at me bemused. There they were with their rosary beads, saying their 'Hail Marys', while this white boy was just sobbing. I can't imagine what they must have been thinking.

Anyway, after a while I hopped onto the moped and went back to the house. Nikita was there making breakfast and I told her what had happened. She started to cry and said, 'What has happened to you? You've totally changed!' Nikita's statement was confirmation of what I already knew; I was born again and there was no going back for me.

A week later Nikita began to believe. She said the sinner's prayer and repented. I was so busy for the Lord I began to get into hard-core preaching on the internet. I was constantly looking at material, learning and posting things on Facebook to send back home. I witnessed about my faith, Christianity and Jesus. All my friends in Wales were worried about me because I had quit drugs and poker overnight. They couldn't comprehend how all this had happened to me.

Nikita and I were still in Goa. One night, I was in my local bar and I was offered some weed and accepted it. I remember getting a quarter of the way down the spliff, then half way and feeling such a hypocrite.

Nevertheless, I continued to smoke the weed and remember hearing voices in my head. These voices weren't the type you can get when you're stoned or drunk. These were voices of reason, the type you get when you give yourself a good talking to or remonstrate with yourself. I remember other thoughts coming into my head that were contradicting my element of faith, in other words contradicting what I knew to be right. This was strange. It wasn't the weed because I'd never known this happen before.

The contradiction against my belief continued so I stopped smoking and said, 'Satan?' All the thoughts in my head went dead. There was a pause and then I heard a voice in my head say, 'what?' followed by laughter, but not the joyous kind. I said 'Satan, that's you isn't it?' A voice said the same thing again, 'what?' in a sort of *'what's your problem?'* manner, followed by more laughing. Satan was laughing at me.

Then the Holy Spirit came over me in a shower. It was almost as if God had wiped the need for the weed out of me. He said, 'Throw it outside at the back of the bar.' So I took the weed I had in my pocket and did as I was told. That was it! I was not going to touch that stuff again.

As the days progressed I continued to learn more and more by listening to ministries and teachings. I wasn't aware of it at first but God was beginning to reveal things to me. I didn't realise what I was doing but God was showing me so many things. I tried to explain spiritual warfare and deliverance to Nikita. I told her that if a demon is cast out from a person and the void is not filled with the acceptance of Jesus Christ as their personal saviour, the demons could return seven fold. She didn't quite understand it.

I was in my mate's bar one night when I had another supernatural experience. There was a guy and his girlfriend there. I'd seen them there before. They both had bad attitudes. God told me that they were possessed, maybe fallen angels in human form. So I prayed silently in my heart. The Holy Spirit came on me again and I felt as if there was a bubble around me, that He was protecting me. In my heart I began to recite Bible verses such as *'Greater is He that is in me than he that is in the world,'* (I John 4:4). I had only been a Christian for a few weeks but the scripture was just prolific.

Amazingly, just from what I was thinking, reciting and the Holy Spirit being around me, this couple began to get very agitated and began to freak out, they didn't like it. I wasn't saying anything out loud. God was speaking into my heart. I continued to silently recite Bible verses then looked at the man and rebuked him in the name of the Lord. He put his hand to his throat and sort of gagged. I rebuked him again and then a third time in Jesus' name and snot came out of his nose. He got up and walked out followed by his girlfriend.

Nikita and I saw this couple in the same bar a few times and when they saw us they would just get up and leave. One night, we got on the moped as usual to go home and realised they were following us so we took a detour and lost them.

I asked Lloyd why he had continued to frequent a place which was clearly dangerous for Christians. He said that he and Nikita had a lot of friends who would meet at this particular bar, it was a popular place and the music nights in particular attracted quite a lot of people.

I think the bar was a meeting place for Satanists or something of that nature, perhaps witchcraft. There was definitely something dark there. On one occasion I tried to pray over the bar to cleanse it. As I prayed silently I noticed that there were some guys that I hadn't seen there before. They got very vexed and a guy got up and moved away from me.

I noticed that the eyes of these men were literally black. One of these guys handed me a card and on the flip side was a picture of a pole with a serpent wrapped around it. I held it in my hand and prayed over it with a look of disgust on my face. It was probably a cursed object so I left it there. It was very strange but I think in some way I was in attracting more of these people.

On music nights at the bar the music was definitely satanic. I could hear voices casting spells on the vocal tracks. On one occasion I saw a woman, who I later discovered was a witch, chanting incantations to herself before she went into the bar.

One night, I saw the same woman bouncing up and down to the music in between some chairs. I felt the warmth of the Holy Spirit and God giving me verses which I recited silently. Suddenly, she began to come towards me but was pushed back onto a chair by an invisible force. It was as if she had hit a force field around me. She tried several times but was unable to get back up again, she was just held there.

God protected us throughout these encounters and instructed us to leave Goa a lot earlier than we had planned to. I don't tell a lot of Christians that part of my testimony simply because they wouldn't believe it. Nikita didn't believe it and she was with me at that time. I told my father and brother-in-law who were also sceptical.

Lloyd and I discussed how some Christians are terrified of demons but we are assured by the Lord that we have nothing to fear. The devil has no power or authority over those who are secure and grounded in Christ. We are bought with a price. The enemy has no legal rights over us. We have complete authority and victory in the name of Jesus Christ. Amen.

'Submit to God, resist the devil and he will flee from you,' James 4:7.

'God hath not given us a spirit of fear but of power, and of love, and of a sound mind,' (2 Timothy 1:7).

9

Claudette Smith

Claudette and her husband Paul both attend the City Temple Church in Cardiff. They have been married for twelve years and have four lovely children. Christalla and I really value the friendship of this God fearing couple. Paul and Claudette are both key members of the church Outreach Team. They demonstrate the great heart they have for the homeless week in and week out by cooking, cleaning, supporting, encouraging, and praying with those who need spiritual support.

This is Claudette's testimony:

When I was growing up I was the victim of systematic physical and psychological abuse. The perpetrator was my father. As a consequence I suffered deep emotional pain which never left me even as I matured into adulthood.

Prior to meeting my husband, I met a man whose name was oddly enough, also Paul. A relationship developed between us and as time went by we decided that we wanted to have a child. Then the problems began as I found that I was unable to conceive.

My doctor arranged for me to have a scan and the problem became evident. I had a massive thyroid on my womb. I was told that if surgery was attempted, the likelihood would be that

I would bleed internally and this would probably result in hysterectomy procedures. We decided not to take the risk.

As the years went by my partner became disillusioned with the situation. He wanted children and the fact that I could not do so put a huge strain on the relationship. The inevitable happened and we parted.

A year later I met a Christian man called Paul. We fell in love and got married. At that time I was a Jehovah's Witness but Paul wasn't. He was vehemently opposed to the theology of the Jehovah's Witnesses' faith.

During the next two years I didn't use contraception but still nothing was happening. Paul and I desperately wanted a baby so I went to see a specialist during the month of November in 2002. I was warned again, as I had been previously, that if I bled internally following surgery, a hysterectomy would have to be performed. An operation to remove the thyroid from my womb was arranged for March 2003.

Then, two months later, the most amazing thing happened. I fell pregnant. During my pre-natal scan it was noticed that two more thyroids had developed in my womb. It was a worrying time and to complicate things further my pregnancy was problematic. We almost lost our first child but thanks to God she survived. Paul and I named her Leticia.

Subsequent scans at the hospital revealed that although the thyroids had reduced in size, they were still there.

I conceived again within a few months but regrettably we lost that child. But, God is good, and He gave us the gift of our second child who born two years after Leticia.

Meanwhile, the doctors at the hospital were keeping an eye on the ever present thyroids. But, praise God, by the time I fell pregnant with the twins there was no trace of the thyroids.

They had all disappeared! This was a miracle. God had heard and answered the prayers of my family, friends and congregation of my church.

Despite God moving so wonderfully in our lives my husband, Paul, still had misgivings about the doctrines of the Jehovah's Witness movement. When I searched my heart I realised that there was a part of me that was in agreement with Paul's concerns, so I left the church.

Several months later, Paul had an invitation to attend the City Temple Church. So, Paul, myself and the children all went along and were immediately smitten. We were home.

During that year I shared the experiences of my early life with a brother in Christ. During our conversation he revealed something to me that transformed my life. He told me that when a person holds unforgiveness in their heart for another, it can stop that individual moving forward with the Lord.

Those words ignited an awakening within me. I suddenly realised that the things of the past were holding me back, but by the grace of God there was a solution to my problem. It was going to be difficult for me to do but I had to forgive my father. I knew that if I found forgiveness in my heart for him, the Lord would forgive me and heal the deep seated wounds within me.

I went to my father's house and opened my heart. I told him that I forgave him for all the hurt he had caused me. I also asked him to forgive me for my anger, and rebelliousness towards him. What happened afterwards was astounding.

Despite knowing that I was in a psychologically bad place, I had not been aware of the extent of the pain and resentment I had been carrying in my mind and body. The full realisation came when I left my father's house. I didn't just walk out, I floated. It felt as if the whole world had lifted off my shoulders.

In the past it had felt as if every step I took forward was followed by a step backwards. Now I felt as if could see the whole world clearly. It was as if the fog of resentment, recrimination and pain had lifted and the sunshine had broken through. I will never forget that life changing experience – it was amazing! My chains were gone, I'd been set free.

Following the breakthrough with my father, I became hungrier for the Lord, I felt my life changing. My strength and confidence grew, it was wonderful. I was finally becoming the woman the Lord put me on this earth to be. The more I read God's word the more He was speaking to me and the more I could hear Him. He anointed me with the gifts of the Spirit and in particular the gift of the word of knowledge. I want to emphasize that all these blessings came to me from the Lord after I forgave my father.

As Christians we don't realise how a spirit of unforgiveness can cause us so many problems. If we don't forgive a brother or a sister, we will never progress in our lives. It will hugely affect our walk with God. He loves us and wants to give everything to us, but we have to obey His word. For me it's one of the most important commands God gives us in the bible.

The relationship between my father and I has grown so much it is almost unrecognisable compared to what it was previously. Now we are very close. Years ago he used to say things that would make my blood boil, the anger and the hate I had for him was so intense that I couldn't stay in the same room with him. Now, however, I can sit with him and have great conversations. Unfortunately, during this period he became ill, but something astounding happened. My father came to me and asked me to pray for him. It was incredible the extent to which the Lord had healed our relationship that he could come to me and ask me to intercede on his behalf. Thank You Lord.

Bless those that curse you, pray for those who ill treat you, (Luke 6:28).

For if you forgive men when they sin against you, your Heavenly Father will also forgive you. But if you do not forgive men their sins, your Father will not forgive you, (Matthew 6:14-15).

Where is Your Faith? – Just Believe!

10

Sherrie Case

August 2012

Sherrie attends the City Temple and is a member of the Outreach Team. At the point of writing Sherrie's story she was about to undertake the *Alpha Course* with a view to learning more about the Lord in preparation for baptism.

I was helping to set up tables in the church foyer area in readiness for the arrival of the homeless guys. As I was doing this I noticed Sherrie wincing in pain as she walked across the foyer with her cane. I felt the Holy Spirit prompt me to ask if she would like prayer for healing. She said that she didn't think praying for her would make any difference. 'I will just have to live with it,' she said. 'No one has to live with pain and sickness,' I replied. 'God doesn't want that, He wants us to be whole.'

As I was speaking to Sherrie someone entered the range of my peripheral vision. It was our Outreach colleague Adey. She was placing some coffee and biscuits on the counter.

'Do you know Adey?' I asked. Sherrie nodded. I told Sherrie that Adey had been prayed for by Pastor Brian Creswell at a Saturday morning meeting at the Llanishen Community Shop a couple of weeks prior and after four years of often excruciating pain had been set free. 'Okay, book me in,' she said.

Later in the evening Sherrie accompanied Christalla and I into the church's auditorium for some privacy. She told us that she had several problems with her legs and was waiting for an operation on her ankle. Sherrie said she needed to use a cane for support whilst walking and was in constant pain.

Christalla and I laid hands on her and began to pray for her. When we came to the end our prayers Christalla enquired how she was feeling. Sherrie said that she was experiencing a warm feeling in her legs and the pain was easing.

In an instant the recollection of a dream I'd had the previous night came to me. In the dream God had instructed me to anoint a man with oil whilst I prayed for him. The man was known to me so I was unsure if God had reminded me of the dream so that we could anoint Sherrie. I decided to go ahead and do it regardless. I told Christalla that I was going to get a bottle of olive oil which is kept in the church for anointing purposes and went off to fetch it. As I returned with the oil I whispered, 'Please heal her, Lord.'

We prayed for Sherrie again during which time Christalla anointed her head. As Christalla was doing so I noticed that Sherrie's body was quivering and then she let out a huge sigh.   I assumed that she was just feeling relaxed but then Sherrie said, 'Something shifted whilst you were praying. I could feel the pain leaving my legs...it's amazing...the pain has gone...thank you!'

Christalla and I told Sherrie to praise God not us and emphasised the importance of giving thanks to the Lord for her healing on a regular basis.

The following day at Sunday night church Sherrie told our friend, Kathy Matthias, that Christalla and I had prayed for her the previous night and she was still pain free.

The following week at Outreach, Sherrie was assisting Adey in the kitchen tidying up at the end of a long and busy evening. She told Adey that in the past she would have been in agony having spent several hours on her feet. However, now she had no pain at all! Thank You Lord.

Where is Your Faith? – Just Believe!

11

Prayer, Ministry and the Homeless

If we don't embrace the power of the Holy Spirit to bring signs, wonders and miracles to the lost, then we are not going to have a means to lead them to the Lord. Jesus said in John 4:48, 'None of you will ever believe unless you see signs and wonders.'

In 1 Corinthians 2:4-5, the Apostle Paul wrote these words in his letter to the church at Corinth, 'My speech and my message were not in plausible words of wisdom, but in demonstration of the Spirit and of power, that your faith might not rest in the wisdom of men but in the power of God.'

When Christalla was divinely healed on the October 4, 2011, God saved her life. As a consequence of this miracle, Christalla and I were freed from bondage, our lives were transformed and our faith was strengthened. God blessed Christalla with abundant health and energy which gave us the opportunity to serve Him in more practical ways. We fully surrendered our lives to the Lord and asked that He use us in the furtherance of His Kingdom on earth.

In January 2012, Christalla and I felt that God wanted us to serve within the City Temple Impact Outreach Project for the homeless. At that time this initiative was being led by Antonio Carvalho, Mandy Powell and Aled Power who had all previously worked on the streets helping the homeless.

Several churches within the city of Cardiff united together with the aim of providing food and overnight shelter for people who were homeless. This was an amazing achievement. Throughout the winter, up to fifteen homeless men and on occasion one or two women (rising to sixty people by March), had a cooked meal and somewhere warm to sleep for each night of the week.

On Outreach nights Christalla and I would invariably be tasked with inflating air beds, changing bedclothes, serving food, tea and coffee. However, as rewarding as that was what Christalla and I most looked forward to doing was our conversations with the guys. We would listen as they related details about their chaotic lifestyles, drug and alcohol addictions, violence, abuse, sickness and mental health problems.

I recall one night in the early days of the project when I walked into the back room which is adjacent to the kitchen, to find Christalla being comforted by two Christian sisters. She was sobbing her heart out. She told me that she could feel the pain in the heart of a young man she had been talking to. He disclosed to her that he had been the victim of systematic sexual abuse as a child. He said that he'd internalised the trauma of this experience and had been carrying this burden for years. He told her that apart from his girlfriend, Christalla was the first person he had ever told about the abuse. She said that she was crying out of compassion for him.

At the Outreach Project we offered the men and women we served hope through Jesus Christ. We would tell them that what were seemingly insurmountable problems could be overcome by His love and compassion for them, if they just called upon His name. *'For whosoever calls upon the name of the Lord shall be saved,'* (Romans 10:13).

As the months progressed Antonio suggested that perhaps we could take things to another level in terms of prayer requests from the homeless and offering the men and women personal prayer sessions.

This idea resonated with Christalla and I because so many of the guys were desperate and broken, so we formed a prayer team. Part of our role was to ask each person if they had a prayer request and then we would write those requests on cards which Christalla and I would collect in a box, collate and then cover in prayer when we returned home that evening. On Sunday mornings at church we would pass copies of the prayer requests to the Pastoral Team for more intercession during weekly prayer line sessions.

Our main role, however, was to encourage individuals to allow us to pray for them either openly or privately. At first we only had a few people take us up on our offer because they were a little suspicious of our motives. Some thought that we would bash them over the head with our Bibles to try and convert them and others just didn't think that prayer would make any difference. However, when the guys became more familiar with us and a measure of trust had been built up, things began to change.

When some of the guys heard that those who had been prayed for felt better for it and some even got healed, the numbers of individuals asking for prayer increased dramatically.

Other members of Outreach Team would also pray with the guys whenever the opportunity presented itself, but despite this Christalla and I had to begin booking people in for prayer and also form a second prayer team to cope with the demand!

Here are a few short stories which illustrate how God moved mightily during the Impact Outreach nights at the City Temple Church in Cardiff.

(Some names in the stories have been anonymised to protect the identities of those individuals. However each person is willing to verify their testimonies if asked to do so.)

September 1, 2012

Outreach Team Member BM arrived at the church hobbling badly. He told Outreach co-leader Mandy Powell that he had been riding his bike home from work when he had a collision with a car. As a consequence the bike was damaged and he sustained a painful knee injury.

Someone offered to convey BM to hospital but he refused. Mandy suggested that he ask Christalla and I to pray for him. BM was reluctant to do so stating that that he didn't think prayer would work. 'Don't you believe that God can heal you?' I asked.

'Not sure,' he replied, but agreed to allow us to pray for him.

BM hopped into the church on his right leg because he couldn't put any weight on the other leg. I asked BM to roll his trouser leg up so that we could inspect the injury. The kneecap was clearly twisted out of position and swollen. We asked him to stretch the leg out between two chairs and began to pray.

After a short while we paused to ask if there any improvement. BM raised his eyebrows to acknowledge his surprise as he managed to flex his knee slightly. 'It feels better,' he said. Encouraged by this response, Christalla and I pressed in with more intercessory prayer. BM bent his knee again and the leg moved more freely. I felt led by the Holy Spirit to anoint the knee and we prayed again. Before we had finished praying BM said, 'The swelling has reduced and the knee has clicked back into place.'

Given that BM had been doubtful that he could be healed, he didn't seem overly surprised at the miracle that had just taken place in front of his eyes. He simply rolled his trouser leg down, stood up, thanked us and limped back into the church foyer.

Christalla and I had faith that BM would recover quickly and thanked the Lord for His wondrous healing power. When we returned to the foyer I excitedly told Mandy what had happened.

Later on in the evening I saw BM go out through the glass doors of the foyer onto the pavement outside. He unlocked his bike and appeared to be inspecting the damage. I went outside to see if I could assist. BM told me that the front wheel was badly buckled so he couldn't ride the bike home, but it wasn't a problem because he was now able to walk without pain. Thank you Lord!

September 8, 2012

Prior to the beginning of the evening session Chris felt led by the Holy Spirit to anoint all the chairs set out for the homeless. Later on team member Lloyd Jelinek introduced me to a guy I hadn't previously met. I will refer to him as RD.

RD told me that he had a bad injury. He pulled up his right trouser leg and pulled down a heavy elasticated bandage which revealed a badly swollen and bruised ankle. RD told me that he had recently had surgery on the ankle but had damaged it further by the means of an accident. He then asked me a question that made me giggle, 'Can you heal this?' I said, 'No, but I know someone who can.'

I suggested that we should all go into the main auditorium and there we would ask God would sort the problem out. RD was reluctant to go at first but decided to relent on the proviso that Lloyd went too. I located Christalla and we took RD into the church to pray for him.

RD's eyes were cold, empty and emotionless. He told us that he was on a mission to die. RD said that he was slowly killing himself by not eating and just drinking strong spirits. 'I believe that we are living in hell,' he said. 'Hell isn't anywhere else, it's here on earth.'

We discovered during conversation that RD was deeply troubled. He'd suffered sexual abuse as a child and would not forgive the perpetrator. Although he believed in God, having being brought up as a Catholic, he did not believe that God could help him. 'No one can get over what was done to me,' he said.

'I wouldn't ask God to do something that I can do myself,' he said. 'You can't do something like this on your own strength,' Christalla said. 'Only God can heal wounds as deep as the ones you have.'

RD also told us that he was troubled by terrible nightmares. Christalla asked him several times to try to forgive the man who committed the abuse against him but he declined to do so.

'Okay,' said Christalla. 'We'll pray for healing for your ankle.' We began to pray then after a short while asked RD how the ankle was. 'Slightly better,' he replied.

I anointed the ankle and we prayed again. Suddenly RD shouted an obscenity and said excitedly, 'The swelling's going down and the bruises are fading. Sorry for swearing but I have just seen a miracle.'

Christalla told RD that she had prayed that God would minister to him in his sleep to soften his heart and show him what he had to do to forgive. She said that she had also prayed that He would reveal someone to show RD that God can heal those who have suffered sexual abuse.

We invited RD to come back to the project in a week's time. I felt led to tell RD that I believed that God would fully heal his ankle to demonstrate His power and that this would happen by the time we saw him again the next week.

Christalla commented that whilst we were talking to RD she had seen darkness around him. 'It was completely black, he was completely surrounded by blackness.'

The following week the Outreach team was preparing to pray when RD walked in and joined our circle. The door was unlocked, which was unusual, so it was a surprise to see him standing there. I went over to him and asked how things were. I immediately noticed that his eyes were brighter, the dark lifelessness had gone. RD shook his head in amazement as he said, 'I witnessed a miracle last week.'

RD told me that the nightmares had stopped and the injury was so much better. 'I'm so grateful for the healing because the injury had caused me so much pain and stress,' he said. 'Being homeless, the police constantly move people like me from street to street and place to place. I was unable to rest my ankle which aggravated the injury. You are a healer you are. I want to thank you and your wife for healing me.'

'Whoa!' I said. 'Stop right there! God is responsible for healing your ankle and the nightmares going away, not us. We are simply the people who pray for you. Give Him the glory.'

Later, during the evening a member of the Outreach team stood up and gave their testimony. As the story unfolded it was revealed that God had healed that person from a life threatening disease but also from the pain of sexual abuse. God answered Christalla's prayer that RD would be shown an example of someone who was divinely healed.

A couple of weeks later RD turned up at the project with his new girlfriend and asked Christalla and I to pray for her. His eyes beamed as he told us that he had brought her along because, 'When you prayed, He (God) touched me.'

RD said that he was currently attending an alcohol rehabilitation project as he was determined to give up alcohol. A few weeks later RD told us the amazing news that the 'rehab' had been successful and he was now free of alcohol. He also told Christalla that he wanted to give something back by joining the Outreach Team.

September 2012

My dear Christian brother, Paul Smith, introduced a man to me who looked a little 'worse for wear'. The poor man had clearly been beaten badly. His eyes were red and bloodshot and he had congealed blood on his ears and face. I was told that he'd been examined by a doctor at the local hospital who told him that he'd received some brain damage from the assault which had included kicks to the head. He already had a speech impediment from birth but the assault had exacerbated the problem to the extent that he could hardly speak at all. Paul told me that his name was ST.

I told him my name but it took what seemed to be an age to reply. At that moment I was asked to assist with bringing some food down from the kitchen. I asked ST if he would like Christalla and I to pray for him later. He nodded enthusiastically.

When my task was completed I began to scan the room to try and locate Christalla. The room was filled with around fifty men and a few women, many were bound by addictions to drugs and alcohol, displaced, broken, and largely despised by society. Yet, here they were in the Lord's house. God was making provision for His lost children with warmth, food and clothes but most importantly they were being shown that He loved them through the Outreach Team. Instead of the looks of disdain and disgust they received on the streets, every hug, handshake, smile and kind word was a witness to God's love, it showed that they mattered. God was demonstrating His bountiful love for His children through us.

I saw the back of Christalla's head through the crowd and made my way towards her. As I approached I noticed that ST was sat on the arm rest of a sofa with his eyes closed whilst Christalla was stood, fervently praying for him. She was flanked by colleagues Paul and Wayne who had their hands laid on him.

Suddenly, ST opened his eyes and effortlessly began to thank Christalla, Paul, Wayne and myself each by name. Thank you Lord!

He began kissing our hands which we stopped immediately. 'Don't thank us,' we said, 'thank God. It's His work not ours.'

As the evening progressed ST's speech deteriorated a little, he wasn't as coherent as he had been prior to prayer. However, we still gave thanks because there had clearly been an improvement.

Three weeks later Christalla and I were both in the City Temple helping out at the Outreach project when a man who looked strangely familiar approached me. His face was lit up with a beaming smile and his eyes were sparkling. As he began to stretch his hand forward to shake mine, it suddenly dawned on me who it was!

He shook my hand warmly and asked if I remembered who he was. He spoke with such confidence and clarity that I began to doubt if he was who I thought he was.

'Yes, I think so,' I said cautiously. 'You…you're the one... who was struggling to speak…ST?' 'Yes, it's me,' he said giggling, 'I'm feeling great.' He told me that as Christalla prayed for him he had felt peace and joy. He said that when his speech briefly returned to normal it wasn't a surprise to him because prior to the assault this would happen if he wasn't stressed or angry.

'I thought the prayer hadn't worked so dismissed it really. However, since that night I have noticed that my speech has improved every day. It's fantastic,' he said.

I explained to ST that divine healing is more often than not a process, it happens in God's time. I thanked God for his compassionate mercy upon ST and called Christalla over. ST threw his arms around her and gave her a huge hug which lifted her off her feet. 'Thank you so much,' he said. 'No,' said Christalla, 'we have to give God the glory, we didn't do it…He did.'

12

How to Keep Your Healing

Despite all the frustration, tears and doubts, I always knew in my heart that Christalla would be healed because I had heard a voice in my spirit tell me so. I knew this was a message from God and shared the good news with Christalla and some Christian friends. One of our friends praised God for this revelation whilst the others smiled supportively. I may have been mistaken but I sensed that some of our friends were hoping that I would be able to cope with the disappointment of what could be just wishful thinking.

I completely understood why they would feel this way because Christalla had not been restored to full health despite the plethora of intercessory prayers that had been said on her behalf over many years.

It is difficult for Christians who believe in a healing God to understand why those we intercede for in prayer are not healed.

There are some who explain this by pointing to obstacles or blockages to healing such as unforgiveness, lack of faith or unbelief in the supplicant. Others abide by the notion that God has purpose in not moving to heal at the specific time we want Him to, because He has a greater plan and His glory will be seen in it.

Our God is sovereign. He has dominion over every living thing. Romans 9:15-21 says…*'I will have mercy on whomever I will have mercy and I will have compassion on whomever I will have compassion…' Therefore He has mercy on whom He wills… but indeed, O man, who are you to reply against God? Will the thing formed say to Him who formed it, 'Why have you made me like this?' Does not the potter have power over the clay?…'*

When God told me He wanted me to write this book, I prayed that He would fulfil the promise He'd made to me that He would heal Christalla. I desperately wanted her to be healed, but wanted to glorify the Lord's name through her testimony within these pages.

Therefore, as an act of stepping out in faith, I set about putting pen to paper and wrote Christalla's story without a conclusion. By the time I had written the second testimony for this book, God had performed the miracle He promised two years earlier, and healed her. God works in mysterious ways which our earthly understanding does not allow us to comprehend. We simply have to accept and trust Him to do it His way.

Some Christians believe in the notion that God makes people sick to punish them, teach them humility, or keeps them that way so that they are dependent upon Him. I completely refute this doctrine. Do you know of any loving, caring parent who would deliberately make their children sick or keep them in pain?

So why would our God who loved the world so much that He sent His only Son, (John 3:16), intentionally make us ill?

Our Father's love is not measurable in human terms. His love is infinitely greater than humanity can ever know while we are on this earth. Why would God send His Son to spend three years undoing what He had put on us and then allow His beloved Son to die in agony? When Jesus hung on the cross, He not only bore our sins, He also bore our sickness and diseases (Matthew 8:17). God would not want us to bear what Jesus has already borne. Sickness and pain is not of God. There was no sickness or disease before the fall of the world.

1 Corinthians 12:9-10 talks about the impartation of the spiritual gifts, *'to another gifts of healing...to another the working of miracles.'* I believe that miracles and healings are a separate phenomenon, miracles happen instantaneously and healings occur gradually.

In my youth (which seems so long ago now) I was a rugby player who suffered my fair share of bumps and bruises. Whenever I had an injury I knew that I would heal eventually and be as good as new. I knew that the cuts and bruises on my body could take a few days or longer to heal, but it would definitely happen.

Supernatural healing works on the same principle. The healing first of all manifests in the spirit before it becomes discernible in the flesh. In other words we don't see the change immediately but it will happen eventually. If you fail to experience a miracle don't be discouraged, healing is progressive, it is a divine process.

Jesus said in Mark 16:18, *'They will lay their hands on the sick and they will recover.'* The government official in John 4:46, who asked Jesus to heal his dying son, received our Lord's assurance that his son would live. As the official was nearing his home, his servants rushed to meet him with the incredible news that his son was recovering.

When God's healing is taking place in a spiritual atmosphere, charged with expectancy, faith runs high. That's the easy part. True belief is tested in a climate of opposition and an often prolonged wait for the full healing to occur.

Doubt begins to infiltrate minds when the healing does not appear to have worked. That is when the enemy sees his opportunity and attacks! Therefore, in order to claim divine healing it is imperative to use the spiritual weapons we have at our disposal; the word of God, faith, worship, praise and prayer.

Some of us will undoubtedly have heard anecdotes about miraculous healings or witnessed God's healing power set someone free, to later discover that the person who had been healed had regressed or the illness had completely returned. Why does this happen?

It is widely documented in the circles of Christians who serve within healing ministries that soon after divine healing has taken place the enemy will seek to destroy what God has miraculously done. Satan cannot undo anything that has been proclaimed by God, however he can trick us into believing our healing hasn't worked. If we are not secure in our faith and belief we become vulnerable to attack. The enemy knows that only good seed that takes root in good soil can produce an abundant yield, so his desire is to steal the Word before it can take root and produce a sustainable healing.

Matthew 13:20-21 illustrates this point thus, *'The man on whom seed was sown in rocky places, this is the man who hears the word, and immediately receives it with joy. Yet he has no firm root in himself, but is only temporary, and when affliction or persecution arises because of the word, immediately he falls away.'*

Following the process of healing we have to affirm and claim the healing through worship, prayer and the word of God. We have to allow His truth to take root in us so that the complete manifestation of healing, from spirit to flesh, can take place.

Prior to her miracle healing at Ffald-y-Brenin, Christalla had experienced divine healings on two previous occasions in 2007 and 2009, only for her illness to inexplicably return. We later discovered that she had unwittingly succumbed to the enemy's deception that her symptoms had reappeared. *So what did she do differently on the last occasion to keep her healing?*

God saved Christalla's life by means of a miracle which removed the life threatening heart and respiratory conditions and also the problematic vertigo and chemical allergy problems.

Prior to leaving Ffald-y-Brenin Christalla bought a booklet entitled *Rhythm of Prayer*. The booklet contained devotional prayers for morning, midday, evening and night. Within the morning set of devotional readings Christalla's eye was drawn to the penultimate prayer which was from *Patrick's Breastplate*,

'Christ as a light illumine and guide me. Christ as a shield overshadow me. Christ under me, Christ over me, Christ beside me, on my left and my right. This day be within and without me, Lowly and meek yet all powerful. Be in the heart of each to whom I speak, in the mouth of each who speaks unto me. This day be within and without me, Lowly and meek yet all powerful. Christ as a light, Christ as a shield, Christ beside me, beside me on my left and my right.'

When we returned to Cardiff that evening, Christalla was led by the Holy Spirit to memorise this prayer and did so within five minutes of reading it. This was an amazing accomplishment because for Christalla to memorise any text was a miracle in itself. A symptom of her condition was very little memory retention of written word, directions, names of individuals etc.

Christalla could watch a movie and forget the plot by the time the credits rolled (if she remained awake long enough). This had been a significant problem to Christalla for over two decades!

That night, whilst Christalla was sleeping, she was woken by chest pain and the sensation of her heart beating wildly. She did not panic and prayed for guidance on how to overcome these symptoms. The Lord responded immediately.

During the next few days the enemy attacked Christalla under the guise of familiar symptoms, attempting to deceive her that they had returned. Christalla would simply place her hand on her heart, repeat the passage and the symptoms would vanish.

Christalla continued to use this process to fend off these attacks and they gradually became less frequent. The enemy eventually gave up, he was defeated. *'In all these things we have the victory through Him who loves us,'* (Romans 8:37).

Christalla received God's divine guidance on how to claim the miracle of her healing. He reminded Christalla of the *Breastplate Prayer* that she had memorised earlier that evening. He told Christalla to speak the words of the prayer whilst placing her hand on her heart and the symptoms vanished immediately! 'However, her body was still weak from years of illness.

So month by month the Lord lovingly restored health to Christalla's body. He spoke to her clearly, instructing her to build up her strength for a period of a year and then she should relinquish her sickness benefit payments. Christalla was obedient to God's instructions but it took quite a step of faith to do so because now that Christalla was healed we were able to get married, but had no money. All my savings had been spent on medical bills and treatments for Christalla. We prayed for a solution. Our God is a faithful God and He answered our prayers for provision in an awesome way. Not only did He give us the time and of date of the wedding, He provided everything we needed. It was a fantastic day shared by 200 people. That demonstrates how good God is and how much He wants to give us good things. Jesus tells us in John 10:10 that He came to give us life and life in abundance. Our Father in heaven wants us to enjoy our time on earth, we just need to ask.

I don't want to suggest that it would be easy for a person who has no other means of support to make the decision to stop receiving benefits. However, a person that Christalla and I know lost their healing because they continued to accept benefits although they were not entitled to. If we put our trust in God He will provide, He always comes through. Philippians 4:6-7 says, that we shouldn't worry about anything but that by prayer and supplication we should make our requests known to Him. Then His peace that transcends all understanding will guard our hearts and minds. We have nothing to fear if we keep our eyes fixed on Jesus.

The Lord proved that He will honour and reward confidence in Him. *'He will watch over His word in your heart and on your lips to perform it,'* (Jeremiah 1:12). Christalla was faithful and obedient; Christalla dared to believe!

The miracle of healing is a gift that God gives us in His desire to restore His children to Him so that they can share His ways and wonders. Here are some healing verses that assure us that the Lord can heal and will heal. Just believe.

❖ *Now to Him who is able to do exceedingly and abundantly above all that we could ask or think according to the power that works in us,* (Ephesians 3:20).

❖ *The things that are impossible with men are possible with God,* (Luke 18:27).

❖ *'For I will restore health to you and heal you of your wounds,'* (Jeremiah 30:17).

❖ *He was wounded for our transgressions; he was crushed by our iniquities; upon Him was chastisement that brought us peace and with his stripes we are healed,* (Isaiah 53:4).

Where is Your Faith? – Just Believe!

144

Epilogue

Father, thank You for showing us Your power, compassion and love through Your divine healing.

Your love brings healing to us in so many ways. We know that whatever happens in our lives Your love will never end. How amazing that You love us so, even though we don't deserve it. I pray for the release of the power of faith and healing for those who want to see a move of God in their lives. Amen.

Some of you reading this book will not have a personal relationship with the Lord. If through reading this book a burning desire to know Him has grown within you and you truly want Him to come into your life, you could pray a prayer something like this:

Heavenly Father, I admit that I have done wrong and need Your forgiveness. I believe that Jesus Christ died for me, paying the penalty for my sins. I am willing right now to turn from my sin and accept Jesus Christ as my personal Saviour and Lord. I ask that You send the Holy Spirit into my life to fill me and help me to be the kind of person You want me to be.

Thank You, Father, for loving me.

In Jesus' name. Amen

Where is Your Faith? – Just Believe!

Welcome to your new journey. I highly recommend that you find a church that feels right for you. A church which has the strong foundations of a community of Christian people, who will help you grow in your walk with God.

Bibliography: This Edition of Daily Prayer, Copyright 2009, Ffald-y- Brenin, Christian Retreat Centre.

I am the Lord that healeth thee

Exodus 15:16

Where is Your Faith? – Just Believe!

Ken Bailey was born in Gloucester, England, to parents who emigrated from the West Indies in the 1950s. After an apprenticeship in the glass industry and later running his own window supply company, Ken changed careers and decided to work in the Criminal Justice System and to that end gained a BA (Hons) in Community Justice at De Montfort University, Leicester. He later relocated to Cardiff, South Wales, in 2005. A year later he met Christalla who is now his wife and they attend the City Temple church in Cardiff.

Since the writing of this book Ken and Christalla have formed 3G Ministries which incorporates: House of Prayer, Healing Rooms and One to One Ministry.

Where is Your Faith? – Just Believe!